BURN PATTERNS

MARTIN PREIB

Cover photo by Unknown

Cover design and interior formatting by Kristen Forbes, deviancepress.com

ISBN 978-1-72-680440-0

This book is dedicated to William B. Crawford.

After continued personal ambition and effort, as a young fellow, to enter with the rest into competition for the usual rewards, business, political, literary, and c. — and to take part in the great *mèlée*, both for victory's prize itself and to do some good — After years of those aims and pursuits, I found myself remaining possess'd, at the age of thirty-one to thirty-three, with a special desire and conviction. Or rather, to be quite exact, a desire that had been flitting through my previous life, or hovering on the flanks, mostly indefinite hitherto, had steadily advanced to the front, defined itself, and finally dominated everything else. This was a feeling or ambition to articulate and faithfully express in literary or poetic form, and uncompromisingly, my own physical, emotional, moral, intellectual, and aesthetic Personality, in the midst of, and tallying, the momentous spirit and facts of its immediate days, and of current America — and to exploit that Personality, identified with place and date, in a far more candid and comprehensive sense than any hitherto poem or book.

— WALT WHITMAN

CONTENTS

PROLOGUE

A small wave pushed my lifeless body into a boulder just offshore. Then with each wave after, I bumped it again and again, until a breeze came along and slowly pushed me around it. Soon, I knew the winds and currents would build as the morning moved into afternoon. They would push me onto the row of boulders that lined the shore of Lake Michigan. I wondered if my body might slip through a crevice in them and I would be hidden from all passersby, students, runners, bike riders. Only the growing stench would indicate my presence. Since I had been a police officer when I was living, I could easily imagine the call coming over the police radio.

"Caller says there is a terrible odor coming from the rocks on the shore off Loyola University."

Then I could imagine the police approaching. I knew they would be my coworkers because I recognized this was the landscape of my old district, the Twenty-Fourth, Rogers

Park. When they approached, their hands would be casually placed in their pockets, their shoulders slumping the way so many patrolmen's did after they got out of the squad car. The sounds of their radios would announce their approach. With their flashlights they would peer down until one ray of light set on me.

"Oh my God. It's fucking Preib," one would say.

"He owes me ten bucks for lunch last week."

"He's got three lockers in the locker room. Three of the big ones. I call dibs on one of them."

"Fucking A. He stinks," the other would say as they pulled their T-shirts over their noses.

I could not remember anything about my time in the lake or how I got there, only a powerful instinct that I wanted to remain in it. Even now I found the floating pleasurable, beautiful even. I liked the slow rise and fall of the waves beneath me, the sound of the seagulls overhead, the morning light off the water and shore. A dread about returning to the city now began to take over. As I came closer to the shore, certain worldly powers returned. I could, for example, see things without turning my head or eyes, and I could hear acutely, even things far away. Unable to move my decaying carcass, I sensed the emergence of increased imaginative powers, things like the ability to spot irony and weave allegories and, with them, a resurgence of memory. And there was language. I found myself thinking in sentences again. They were all devices, I concluded, that would be of great use in the coming days. It was as if the now formidable physical limitations of being dead were compensated by greater, more penetrating insights than when I was living.

The imaginative insights included images and voices of loved ones, so exact, so authentic, that it was almost unbearable. Even now just offshore, I could hear my mother's voice, and then my father's. Off to the south was the church at Loyola where my mother had played the organ eight decades earlier. The memory initiated the faint sound of music, Mozart. Was that my mother? As the notes filled me, I wondered if my father could have imagined in the years after WWII that his youngest son would return to his childhood neighborhood as a cop and patrol it. Irony, always a powerful force in the city, was now piercing in its power to illuminate.

If things already got this intense offshore, what would it be like when I finally washed up on the sand, when they took me in an ambulance to the hospital or to the morgue? I dreaded the hullabaloo after the discovery of my body. More police cars would arrive, the fire department, a crowd, many of them students at Loyola. Then I would be hauled to the morgue. No need to sugarcoat that; I had seen many autopsies. There was more to my dread than that, though. I had learned when I was alive that Chicago has a peculiar power over its dead, one that holds even the deceased in its corruption.

This power over the dead, particularly those murdered, had pulled me in and was, I sensed, a primary factor in my current state. The murders were tied to the year I first returned to Chicago in 1982, after our family moved away when I was a child. In that year was a collection of murders that would transform the city. Some involved the murders of police officers. Others were ghetto murders that were resurrected in the city's crooked institutions and transformed the cases from what the courts had called them into something completely opposite; murderers transformed into victims, heroic cops into criminals, the incarcerated set free, the innocent incarcerated. These transformations were like some magical force had taken control of the city, a force over living and dead. As I grew more intimate with these murders and saw their interconnectedness, these killings enveloped me. Now I was caught up in them, my body pulled from the peaceful waters of Lake Michigan back to the city. There was nothing I could do about it.

My return, therefore, was not accidental; it was fateful. The city would not let me go where the dead normally went. It was holding me. It had pulled at me while I was living, but now, in my death, held me firmly. Talk about fucking clout. I had no idea what was in store for me, but none of it seemed good. Man, did I wish the current would take me out again, but I knew it wouldn't.

I could hear some boat engines farther out on the lake, car doors slamming on the streets near the beach. There were some voices of Loyola students going to early classes. Soon my body would be hauled out of the water. There was nothing that could be done, so I stopped trying to move my arms and legs, and let the waves push me in. While I waited, I tried to piece the whole story together again, in a manner that was straight, without any taint of corruption, just as I had tried when I was living, wondering at the same time if this was the very reason the city would not let go of me.

Chapter 1

SCOOTER

I was stuck at a red light on my scooter, just north of downtown. The wind shot down the opening of my coat into my chest. My hands were freezing on the handlebars. Taxis careened in front of me. I had underestimated the time it would take to travel on a scooter from the far North Side of Chicago to Hyde Park on the South Side, where the University of Chicago resides. I was already running late for a meeting with an editor at the university press there, late for an interview about publishing my first manuscript. When I started out, it was sunny and warm, but as I drove down Clark Street, clouds appeared and the temperature dropped. Winds picked up. Because the scooter was underpowered, I didn't dare take it onto Lake Shore Drive. Traveling down smaller streets took much longer than I figured. I had to stop every few blocks for buses, traffic lights, and congestion. The manuscript, a half-finished draft, was rolled up in my backpack and held together by a rubber band. In it were several essays, with a great deal of storytelling, about picking up dead bodies and hauling them to the morgue when I worked the wagon in the far north neighborhood of Rogers Park, where my mother and father had grown up. One chapter, the first one, had already been published. The others had not. I could feel the slight weight of the manuscript on my back. *How unprofessional*, I thought, when I shoved it into the backpack at the beginning of the trip that morning. What would it look like when I pulled it out of the backpack at a restaurant, all rolled up, with creases in it? Would the peanut shells and wrappers at the bottom of my backpack also spill out onto the table?

I glanced at a clock on the dashboard of a car that rolled by. Perhaps I was too late already. We stopped at a light. I looked at myself in the reflections of cars. The windows exaggerated my features, giving ludicrous expression to my incongruity. I was a cop and a writer on a scooter headed downtown, late for an appointment I should never have been late for. The distortions in the windows, though false, seemed more truthful than my real image, living metaphors. The light changed. I couldn't accelerate fast enough because the scooter motor was so weak. Cars, trucks, and buses rode right up on my ass, some honking, startling me and causing me to swerve a bit. I could see the angry faces of drivers when they eventually passed. The revving of the engine generated too much heat. I watched the temperature gauge approach the red warning section. When I crossed the metal grating of the State Street Bridge, the tires got caught in the grooves and pushed me left and right. The sharp winds over the river made it worse. I feared I would be thrown under one of the buses or trucks around me. Worse, I thought I might be pushed to the edge of the bridge and then over, into the cold water below. If I did fall into the river, I decided I would not try to get out. I would let the current take me wherever it went. While floating, I could watch the rescue vehicles approach as my consciousness dimmed. I was hopeful I would freeze to death before they fished me out. I could see myself looking up from the water, at the bridge, the landscape of the city, the immense buildings, taking it all in as the cold slowly put me to sleep. I could not deal with being pulled out and explaining myself to reporters. What was a Chicago cop doing riding a scooter off a bridge into the Chicago River? What's more, what were all these sheets of paper doing floating around him in the water? Was it an accident or a suicide attempt? How should I know? My manuscript would likely not survive. The backpack was weighted down with other heavy objects, so it would sink. Even if it could be recovered, the ink would be corroded and anyone searching in it for answers about my absurd death would be disappointed.

Construction forced traffic to stop on the bridge. I put my feet down and looked left and right, feeling a slight shake caused by the heavy trucks rolling in the opposite lanes. I was right over the water. Looking down, I became disoriented. I focused my vision to see what direction the current moved, but couldn't tell. If I fell off into the water, I wanted to be carried out to Lake Michigan. There was the deep blue and green of the lake when the sun hit it. I could be carried to some lonely beach with only the sound of the waves and seagulls. That would be terrific. Perhaps some animals could eat me, and I would just remain some dumbass who fell off the bridge whose body was never found. But what if the current took me up the river, deeper into the city? There were all those different branches of the river, like arteries of an obese man, the tributaries dirty, clogged with junk-food wrappers, polluted, winding around for miles and miles, passing under busy streets. There were rats swimming these arteries, junkies hiding near them where they could sleep or get high. Maybe I would be carried into a cache of other dead bodies gathered somewhere upriver, joining with other people who shared a similar fate. Perhaps there were piles of such bodies no one had ever discovered.

Traffic began moving slowly past the bridge, snapping me out of my reverie. I was downtown. It was getting even colder and the streets were more congested than I expected. I thought about giving up again, heading home. Neon signs caught my attention. A Vienna Beef sign was lit up in a wonderful yellow. I could smell the aroma of the sandwiches in the exhaust coming from the roof. It was fucking unbeliev-able. It would be so easy to park the scooter between two cars. How fine to get a cup of hot coffee in my hand and a huge sandwich with the beef spilling over the side on a tray with onions and a huge serving of fries. I'd get large fries for sure. Put a big mound of ketchup next to them and have at it, scooping several of them in the condiment, like a mop, after taking huge bites of the greasy sandwich. Afterward, I could get an early afternoon beer at a bar overlooking the river. I'd get tipsy, then full-on drunk, that wonderful early afternoon drunk that knows you can stay into the evening and the night, that you can drink for twelve or fourteen hours straight. How 'bout that? Buy a little whiskey, neat, to sip slowly with the beer and warm up my bones from the cold ride. I'd leave the manuscript on the bar stool after telling a bunch of lies about myself to the bartender and the crowd, then head home, swerving on the scooter, cursing people out, and giving them the finger. Fuck you, motherfucker.

Should I?

A familiar self-loathing came over me. Why would I fuck up so badly, be so self-destructive that I would undermine my own chance at publishing? If any friend or coworker knew I was late for this meeting, they would have looked at me stupefied. All I ever talked about was writing and being published. I shifted my shoulders, felt the slight weight of my rolled-up manuscript again. The University of Chicago rose up in my mind, a storied, ancient university, and I was late for a meeting that would stamp my name on it, however insignificantly. The many failed comings and goings of my life took shape, the wanderings without destinations, without any clear plans, the ignominy and disappointment. My father's voice emerged, a scathing attack not merely of the fact that I was late, but that I even entertained the idea of getting published. I could hear it coming in every sound from the street. I pulled over on State Street downtown, sensing I was halfway between a destination and decision at the same time.

I lived a largely furtive life. I was enamored with the covert, the secret and hidden places. In my imagination, this was where the compelling things lingered. I wondered if perhaps this was one reason I became a cop, because being a cop put you in the middle of the city's daily subversion and

forced you to figure out the laws that governed this subversion, this living corruption. When I began writing stories
about hauling dead bodies to the morgue—some of whom
were murder victims—this wandering of the secret places
intensified, because I was now roaming the crime scenes in
the city, and I liked the power of the language that came from
it. So too, apparently, did the editor at the University of
Chicago Press, who was now waiting at a South Side diner
for me. There was another aspect of the furtive life I was
living in. Cops in Chicago were accused of all manner of
torture and deception, as if we were the criminals. The
public looked suspiciously at us, wondering what kind of
crime we had participated in, believing that we were racist,
that we had framed someone. I could feel their eyes pass over
me slowly when I was introduced to someone at a party. My
real fear, the one I had not even admitted to myself yet, was
that I didn't want to lose my furtiveness, my sense of living in
the underground. I feared an explosion into legitimacy, and
this was why I had made myself late, why I was pulled into
distorted shapes in the windows of cars idling all about me.
But I gave my word that I would meet with the editor, so I
looked left, then right, turned the throttle, and continued
south, not sure how much farther I would venture.

After Printer's Row, State Street becomes less congested.
Then I entered the South Loop. Here is where the Ickes
projects once stood, the first projects I ever entered when I
started working the street as a cop. This was where I wrote
my first case report for aggravated battery, for a woman who
stabbed her husband. It was the first time I ever wrote the
facts on a case report in a filthy apartment with people

screaming at each other, the radio blaring. It was so confusing, so hard to concentrate; I wondered if I would be able to
do it. The next morning, as we waited for the detective, my
training officer read over my case report narrative, said, "This
is good." I was ecstatic.

Now most of the buildings were knocked down. Develop-
ment was coming. With the road less congested, I could also
see clearly at each intersection. I turned the throttle again. As
I approached each intersection, I slowed down. But if it was
clear, I went right through it, block after block. It was at this
point I finally made the decision that I would meet with the
editor after all, no matter how pissed off he was that I
was late.

It was a few moments later that I saw the red and blue
lights in the mirror on my handlebars. I pulled over, certain I
would get out of the ticket once I told the patrolmen I was a
cop and flashed my ID. But as I looked into the mirror again,
I saw an older male get out, wearing a white shirt with gold
on it. He was a deputy, one of the highest ranks in the police
department. I was good and fucked now, I thought. How
would I explain myself, riding a scooter and blowing through
one light after another? What would he think about a
middle-aged cop speeding on a scooter that was too small for
him? My heart sank as I turned off the scooter. I should have
stayed home. I could be drinking coffee and writing at that
very moment. I could feel the wind. My hands were swollen
and red from the cold. *Best not to tell him I'm a cop*, I thought.
Best just to see how pissed he is. If he was going to write me tickets, he'd have to call a patrol car over. Deputies didn't carry
ticket books.

"What's going on, man?" he said, in a southern black accent.

"Well, sir, I'm kind of in a hurry. I have to be somewhere about a half hour ago, somewhere in Hyde Park."

"Yeah, but you are blowing off every light on the street. I counted five of them," he said.

"Yes, sir. I know."

He looked at me. I decided to try being somewhat honest.

"Well, sir, the truth is that I have a meeting with an editor at the University of Chicago Press about publishing my first book, but like an idiot I am running late. I didn't take into account how bad the traffic would be, and now I'm afraid I'll blow this opportunity."

"Your first book, huh?"

"Yes."

"Well, that is important. Just slow it down and don't blow the lights, okay?" he said as he walked back to his car.

"Yes, sir."

I turned the scooter back on, going the speed limit, until I spotted him in my rearview mirror turn eastbound, then I hit the gas and began running the lights again, certain that behind every creative enterprise there is something essentially illegal at its core.

When I arrived at the restaurant, there was a man sitting in the corner, thin and bookish. I was filled with two contradictory emotions at the same time. On the one hand, I was late, very late for the meeting I had requested. On the other, I had already been through many fruitless arguments with agents and publishers who had told me no one would publish a collection of essays by an unpublished writer. I had come to disagree with them and stood by the value of the essays. To me, these editors, agents, and publishers were often condescending in their manner toward me, and I was weary of it. Would I get another lecture from this editor? This was, after all, the University of Chicago Press. After such a long trip downtown, I wouldn't stay long if I detected any condescension coming from him, if he talked down to me in any way. I walked up with my hand outstretched. He gave back a warm smile and waved me to the seat. He wasn't angry at all. In fact, he thanked me for coming down. Coffee came, and I warmed up. His name was Robert. He didn't seem to want to talk about the book that much, so we talked about writers and about our connections to Chicago. He was completely down-to-earth. He told me he grew up in Mount Greenwood, an enclave of firemen, cops, and other city workers on the far South Side of the city. His father had been a captain with the Chicago Fire Department. *Mount Greenwood, fire department*, I told myself. *What is this guy doing at the University of Chicago?* I relaxed, ate a nice meal as our conversation flowed. By the end of the meal, after a pause in our conversation, he sat back.

"So look, I've read some of your stuff and I really like it. I'd like to offer you a book contract."

Chapter 2

FATHERS AND SONS

I got into my squad car and headed out of the district on what felt more and more like some covert mission. It was a few years after my meeting with Robert. The manuscript was finished. I had moved on in my job, as well, no longer transporting bodies to the morgue. Now I was a regular patrolman in the same district. Robert called me earlier that day and told me he had a few advance copies available for me. It would be the first time I saw the book I had been working on for six years, something physical, palpable after all my labor. It was something I could pick up and show people. *Here it is. Look.* I told Robert to call me when he got home and I would try to get over to his house to pick it up, even though I would be at work in uniform. While in roll call, I got a text message from Robert. He was home and he had the advance copies.

How could I manage taking a squad car to Robert's house? I would have to drive south and west and back again, from Rogers Park, through Edgewater, Lakeview, and then west and farther south, right in the middle of a shift. The route to Robert's house was long and cumbersome, at a time when traffic was congested. Would my sergeant let me go and cover for me? I calculated the odds. I was working alone that day, a good thing. There would be no skeptical partner who needed to be cajoled into such a strange and risky adventure. My squad car listed my district on the beat tag outside, so bosses driving by would know I was far out of where I was supposed to be working. It could get even worse. What if someone along the way wanted police service? I didn't even know the right channels on my radio for all the districts I would pass through. How would I call something in on the radio? Other scenarios came to mind. What if I got in an acci-dent? What would I say if an inspector stopped me, seeing I was out of my district? Still, I decided I would risk it. I turned over various lies I could present to my sergeant to manipu-late him into letting me go. Doctor's appointment? Test results? Gang intelligence? None of it sounded good. The hell with it. Just tell him the truth. My sergeant listened without interrupting as I told him I wanted to pick up my book. He had heard me talking about it for years. He looked at me, paused, then said, "Okay, go ahead."

As I drove through the neighborhood where my parents had grown up, an interview with a writer came into my mind, an interview I had heard some fifteen years earlier. This writer taught his students a trick for finding their voice. He told them that everyone has a certain person in mind they are writing to. Clarify who that person is, he said, and you will hone your voice. As soon as the writer said this, it imposed a clarity for me: that person was my father. As soon as I admitted this, my writing seemed to become clearer. Knowing that you write with a certain person in mind reveals how critically this person has influenced your life, how their voice influences every decision you have made. So it was with me. I could always hear my father's voice echoing in my life, more so as I began writing full-time. I could perceive his voice haunting me in all my furtive movements, including my decision to return to Chicago, his hometown. When I transferred to the North Side from the South Side, the only district open was Rogers Park, where he and my mother had grown up. It seemed fateful when I was transferred there, for my mother had just died, and my father would die soon after I returned to their neighborhood. I had this eerie feeling that my father had somehow been responsible for my return to his neighborhood, including the fact that I was assigned to haul bodies as soon as I got there. Our relationship was such that I felt he enjoyed imposing this dark duty upon me. It seemed as if his ability to force me into hauling the bodies in his neighborhood was a kind of betrayal, a derailing of my private designs as a police officer into a world of his creation, for the hauling of the bodies so soon after he and my mother died was on some days almost impossible to bear; it brought out his voice in my life with such intensity, such over-whelming authority. Why couldn't I have ended up in a district disconnected from my father?

This sense of betrayal, this tying me up in his world even after he was deceased, had the force of the universal about it. Chicago is a living conspiracy, passed on from generation to generation, from fathers to sons. I had become aware of this conspiratorial fate in my own life, pulled back to Chicago, ending up a hauler of dead bodies. And so from the windows of the buildings we passed as we drove the wagon to pick up another body, I felt my father staring down at me and smiling as he watched me wrestle a heavy, leaking, uncooperative body into the rear of the wagon. Sometimes I could even hear his voice, a little bit sneering.

"Hauling dead bodies at forty, huh?"

Not today, though. As the winter dusk came over the city, I drove through the district not to pick up bodies, but to retrieve advance copies of my book. I sensed my father's confusion, his utter bewilderment at the confidence I exuded, at such unexpected fulfillment. My father's face bore a quizzical expression that loomed over me from the red brick buildings. He was wondering, *Where is he going now? Why is he leaving the district?* I felt a turning now, my father's disapproval of everything I had become, disapproval that had overwhelmed me in the days I carried the bodies into the wagons, turned to puzzlement. And I enjoyed it. I enjoyed it a great deal.

There seemed no good route. I'd go south for a while, then west, but each road was thick with traffic, delivery trucks, and buses. It was taking too much time. Here I was again, I thought, living my furtive life, flitting about the city on another half-baked adventure that could get all fucked up, especially if I saw an inspector. As my confusion and anxiety grew, I could feel my father, still puzzled about my trip, watching and enjoying my growing anxiety.

This is gonna be great, he was thinking.

I imagined getting stopped by an inspector.

"Officer, why are you two districts away from where you are supposed to be?"

"Well, I'm on my way to see my editor."

"Your what?"

"My editor. You see, sir, it's really simple, and kind of funny if you think about it. I wrote a book about hauling dead bodies to the morgue, but it's really about my father and other things. You see, I use the stories as a metaphor, well, really an allegory to be exact . . ."

"What the fuck are you talking about? You shouldn't be over here. You're out of your district."

"Yes, yes, that's true, and technically you are right," I could hear myself saying, talking too much with my hands. "But, you see, I had to. I worked on the book for six years. I hauled dead bodies. My father is dead. From the upper floors of buildings, he was watching me carry the dead bodies. He put me there. He did, not me. In Rogers Park. My editor has advance copies of my book. I wrote it. The University of Chicago Press. I rode my scooter and got pulled over. The deputy let me go. There were no tickets. Red lights. I'm getting old. Can't you fucking understand?"

Then I could see the inspector lean into his microphone.

"Squad, I need an ambulance at Kedzie and Montrose for an officer. This may be a mental health transport."

Finally, I found Robert's street and turned down it. A squad car in front of the house and then a uniformed cop walking up to his door was something he probably didn't want the neighbors to see, so I parked a few doors down and hustled up to his front door. Inside Robert handed me two copies of the book, then asked me to sign two of his own. After a few perfunctory photos of fake handcuffing his toddler—"My wife will love this," he said—I walked back to the car. In it, I sat down and stared at the cover image, a wagon in an alley. Then I opened up the first pages. I read the dedication to my mother, another to my friend who advised me, and a Whitman quote on another page. If someone had told me five years earlier I would be a published author, I would have laughed. Glowing with a peculiar kind of joy tinged with melancholy, I placed the books on the dashboard and made my way back to Rogers Park, picking up the top book at every red light, every delay in traffic. It almost felt foreign to me, as if someone else had written it. Slowly I headed north and east, hoping the dispatchers or a boss wasn't looking for me in the district. As I came within a few miles of the district, I cleared myself so I could take any jobs, but there were none.

Back in the district, the euphoria over my book moved quickly, too quickly, into a familiar desolation and sense of loss, as if I had given up more in writing it than I had gained in its realization. This sense of loss came over me, drowning out any sense of accomplishment. Up Sheridan I went, then left on Touhy, by the property where my mother's home had once been. I pulled over. How thrilled she would have been to see my book in print. As I sat there, I felt that I could suddenly hear her voice clearly, could envision her walking in her youth down the street on her way to the lakefront. Then I recalled her slow descent into ill health, and then dementia, just before I was hired on to the police department and hauled dead bodies from her old neighborhood, all of which had been the soil of the book. I vainly fought back the tears remembering the years of my mom's decline. Without thinking about it, I put the car in gear and drove south on Ashland, then east toward Sheridan, circling around until I passed by the apartment on Albion where my father had grown up. I pulled to a stop. I grabbed one of the books from the dashboard again, fanning the pages. There was nothing in me at that moment worried about critical response to the book. At that point, I didn't care.

My father was somewhere behind a curtain in one of the buildings, watching me. I didn't bother to look up and locate him. It was enough to sense he was there. His glance was, no doubt, puzzled, wondering why I had come to seek him out directly, why I was confronting him. Usually he looked for me, and I tried to evade his gaze. But he did not say anything. I waited until I felt certain I had his full attention, as if he were waiting to hear what I said. Then I brought my book up into his line of sight, where I figured he could make it out and see that I was fondling it with some bravado, with some hubris, for my father was a deep reader all his life, with excellent taste. "Not a total bum," I said to him, angrily, sorrowfully.

Chapter 3

OUT EAST

The day was disintegrating, and, with it, I feared, I was as well. I didn't know where I was, what direction to take. There was a slight hill ahead of me, the bed and breakfast I had checked into the day before, back the other way. The early morning started out with such exhilaration, such possibility, and now, as it turned into late morning, I was completely desolate. The autumn chill had left. It was growing hot and I was sweating beneath my dress shirt and slacks. I was in Albany, New York, retracing, as best I could, the landmarks listed in a collection of novels that had so consumed me for most of my adult life that it seemed to me they comprised approximately one-half of whatever literary imagination I possessed. Now I was lost amidst the familiar names of the various streets, government buildings, and the hotels. Though I had just finished writing my first book, I was sinking into a world of complete self-loathing. I had flown to Albany the previous day to meet the writer who had most influenced my life, William Kennedy, the writer who was, in my mind, the pioneer of the American version of a larger literary movement known as magical realism. The other great magical realist was Latin American writer Gabriel García Márquez, whose short stories had been a kind of road map for me as a writer.

The irony was not lost on me that Kennedy's most influential novel, the one that had won the Pulitzer Prize, was the story of a bum and former professional baseball player named Francis Phelan, who returned to Albany to confront his demons, many of whom were ghosts of people he had killed. Francis wandered the town, lost, desolate, just as it seemed I was this very morning. Though I had never been to Albany before, it was a kind of home for me because I had lived in Kennedy's books for so long. As Francis slowly moved back toward the home and family he had abandoned, ghosts took shape in front of him, just as my demons began to rise up now. On the bus, in the bars, Francis faces these ghosts and their accusations. This melding of the real and the fantastic, this was magical realism. In it, the purpose of the fantastic, like introducing dead people as characters, was aimed at reinforcing realism, making it more whole and meaningful.

I lived in Kennedy's shadow; I had been reading Kennedy's novels every day since the early 1980s. When I got stuck in my own writing, I often picked up his novels for clues on how to push onward. I remember a time I was living in Ravenswood and I had sent Kennedy a thirteen-page essay about his novel *Quinn's Book*, which got mixed reviews. I felt as if the critics did not understand the novel. The whole thing made perfect sense to me, so I wrote Kennedy a letter that ended up taking almost two years to write, arising every morning to hammer it out. It turned out to be thirteen pages. Writing it forced me to sort out the reason why his books spoke so much to me. Along the way, I had to master the elements of language, grammar, and punctuation. I remember the Chicago winter I began writing the letter, staring out my apartment window from my desk with an old Sears typewriter on it. This was the first time I experienced the writer's life, and I loved it. I sent the letter, now an essay, to him, and he wrote back saying I got it just right. I pulled his letter out of my mailbox when I was on my way out, going to the el station to catch a train downtown, and I felt as if I were flying above the city as I held the letter in my hand. It seemed to announce: *You are legitimate.*

Kennedy and I met several times over the years, mostly at book readings. Each time, Kennedy asked me if I was writing, and on the occasions I admitted I had given up, I was filled with shame. Later, on the eve of his publishing another novel, I even flew to New York City to interview him. It was an awkward affair, meeting him in his hotel room across from Central Park, me stumbling over my questions much of the time. The questions all boiled down to one desperate plea: *How? How do you write?* But now, with a book under my belt, I had sent him several of my essays, and he praised them, told me to come out for a visit. And so I did, scheduling a kind of literary vacation just before my book hit the general public. I planned a visit first to Albany to see Kennedy, then on to Camden, New Jersey, across the river from Philadelphia, where I would visit the home of Walt

Whitman, the poet who comprised the other half of my imagination.

Now that I was actually in Albany, everything seemed to be falling apart. Kennedy was supposed to contact me that morning, and he, along with his wife, would meet me for the afternoon. But no call had come through, no message. I walked from downtown up a long hill, seeing the streets I had been reading about for years, wondering if Francis Phelan, the broken-down ballplayer haunted by his demons, had walked this road as well. My own demons came. Who was I to think that a writer of Kennedy's stature would want to meet with me? Probably he was dreading it and decided against it. Probably, I figured, as the full desolation set in, he hadn't liked my writing at all. He was only being polite and friendly to a fan. Certainly, as the morning wore on, I figured, he had forgotten all about it. A strong hunger came over me. I walked into a diner that had once been a railroad car and silently ate a lousy BLT sandwich, about ninety percent bread. Afterward, I figured, I would go back to the bed and breakfast where I was staying, read some of Kennedy's novels, take a nap, then hang out until I went to sleep. In the morning, I would rent a car and begin the long drive to New Jersey to see the Walt Whitman House. But now I wondered if there wouldn't be some clusterfuck on that end of the trip as well.

As I came out of the diner into the hot sun, I admitted that there had always been some problem between the magical realists and me, some bridge I had never been able to cross. It had haunted me all my literary life. I could not, for example, embrace fiction, the literary form that had, in my mind, been the most artful and beautiful form that magical realism had taken. For years I had attempted to write fiction about Chicago, but it had never come to anything. Fiction seemed too removed, too opaque for the intensity of the city. It was one reason, I figured, I gravitated as much to Whitman, whose poetry was largely written in the first person about his own time and place. Whitman's poetry was raw and pure, devoid of the art displayed in the magical realists. But there was also another nagging doubt about the magical that disturbed me, one I could not yet put into words. The magical in Chicago did not hold, as it did in Kennedy's fiction and in that of the Latin American writers like García Márquez who were the founders of the movement, the joy and possibility of the magical. In Chicago, what was magical was a black magic, rooted in the city's violent crimes, and there seemed in it an evil intent and a grand deception. My dire view of Chicago's magical world intensified as I became a cop. Walking around downtown Albany, this divide between the magical realist writers and me seemed more palpable, to be moving to the forefront, so much so it seemed to make sense that this meeting with Kennedy would fall through, and that I, walking around the city he had merged into his novels, would fail to connect.

One problem I had with magical realism was its connection to revolution, particularly the Cuban revolution under Castro. The notion that a collection of rebels walking through the jungle could eventually take over the country and take on the world's greatest superpower had infused the collective imagination of that region, then the power of its writers seduced much of the rest of the world, including me.

García Márquez himself was devoted to the revolution, was friends with Castro, and often stayed with him when he traveled to Cuba. In his interviews, García Márquez spoke about socialism being the answer to Latin America's problems, that it was inevitable. Because of his politics and his friendship with Castro, García Márquez was barred from the United States for many years.

Every writer who writes about a specific place lives in a kind of fever, one in which he burns to find the right images from that place and then arrange them with the right words. The connection between magical realism and revolution had come to bother me, for here I was a devotee of this literary movement, rooted in Cuba's Marxist revolution, and I was a cop in a big American city. In fact, I was a cop in a city where revolutionaries and the police clashed infamously during the 1968 Democratic Convention. That clash had reverberated about the city, rearranging it in ways that endured even to my own years on the job. As a cop, I was, through the obligations of my office, opposed to any revolution, especially a Marxist one. I enforced the laws of private property, the free-market system, and democratic processes. I didn't overthrow any systems; I reinforced them. At least I was supposed to. But there was more to my doubts about magical realism than that. As a cop, more and more of what seemed fantastic about Chicago, the kind of fantastic that would call out to the magical realists and the Marxists, seemed evil to me. More so, it often lost the veneer of the magical, revealing itself as a no-good, dirty trick, criminal in nature. How was I ever going to be a writer in Chicago, a legitimate one, devoted to a literary movement whose revolutionary tenets were unraveling in front of me, both as a cop and a writer?

Outside the diner, full from a lousy lunch, a decrepit sandwich from a part of the country where a full-bodied sandwich overflowing with meat and condiments was once held sacred, I walked out into the sun, sensing without the words yet available to me that the fires of revolution that drove the magical realists were something altogether different for me, a cop/writer in Chicago. I sank lower into the desolation not only of a writer who has lost his way, but a writer from Chicago who has lost his way in a foreign city where the greatest magical realist in the country lived and had blown me off. It didn't get much lower than that. Perhaps I should toss the entire trip, go to a bar, book a flight home, and creep back to my most crooked city. Right then, my cell phone rang.

"Hello," I said to William Kennedy, in Albany, on the very streets he had been writing about for more than five decades.

"Hello," he said. "Is this Marty?"

"Mr. Kennedy," I stammered.

"Bill . . ." he reminded me. "I'm so sorry. I lost my cell phone and I had to wait until I got another so I could call. I hope I didn't keep you waiting too long."

"Oh, no, not at all. I've just been wandering around Albany, seeing the sights," I lied, not hinting at my near-suicidal state.

"How 'bout my wife and I pick you up? We are on our way back to the city from a reading. Are you near your hotel?"

"Sure, no problem," I said, miles away from my lodgings.

I flagged down a taxi, headed back to the bed and break-fast. I changed my shirt and brushed my teeth, and then William Kennedy pulled up in a Chrysler LeBaron with his wife. He said we should go to his house, the house he had purchased while scouting a location for one of his books to be turned into a movie with Francis Ford Coppola. Kennedy and Coppola were scouting it because it was the location where the famed gangster Legs Diamond had been murdered by two cops. Kennedy had written a novel, *Legs*, based on the life of Diamond early in his career, and Coppola was making a movie based on the book. While approaching the house's owner about shooting a scene there, the owner offered to sell the house to Kennedy. Now Kennedy wanted us to go back there, and I spent an after-noon in the living room of Kennedy's home, where we talked about film, literature, and dialogue. At one point, I asked Kennedy to show me his writer's studio where he had written my favorite novel, *Quinn's Book*.

"I wrote that one in this room. This used to be my office until I moved upstairs," he said.

"You mean to tell me I am sitting in the room where you wrote *Quinn's Book*?" I said. I began fanning my arms as if pushing some unseen vapor toward my head.

"C'mon, magical realism," I said, and Kennedy laughed.

But the gulf I sensed between Kennedy's world and mine emerged during our meeting. Somehow the subject of former members of a group called the Weather Under-ground, who had spent the 1970s calling for a revolution and setting off bombs throughout the country, came up. Kennedy announced casually that he knew one of the founding members, a Chicago man named Bill Ayers, said they were friends. There was a tense silence when Kennedy told me of his friendship with Ayers, as I, a Chicago cop, was one of the "pigs" Ayers and his group had once announced they wanted to kill. It was a glimpse of the sympathy for violent revolutionaries that permeated magical realists, like García Márquez's friendship with Castro. But I let the subject go and moved on. Why get into a political debate with one's literary hero? Soon our conversation returned to the burdens of good dialogue and our favorite writers. Later we parted company outside Kennedy's home. Kennedy offered me a ride, but I wanted to walk down the streets of Albany after spending the afternoon with the man whom I thought was the greatest writer of the last century in his own hometown.

But even after such a thrilling meeting with a literary hero, my alienation from magical realism not only remained, it intensified. What was once a gnawing doubt had now become a large obstacle in my life: I was in love with a literary movement I could not embrace.

The following day I arose early to head downtown and get a rental car for the long drive to Camden, New Jersey. From Albany I hit the road, following the instructions carefully. Before leaving, I called the Walt Whitman House and told its caretaker I would be arriving around one o'clock. Without the GPS I had recently purchased, I never would have made it, there were so many interstates crisscrossing. Even when I got the route wrong, the navigator told me how to turn around. At one point, it even told me to take an alley, and it worked.

Camden was right across the river from Philadelphia. In Whitman's day, it was a bustling city, central to many of the railroads. Now it was a ghetto. The plan was to spend the day at Whitman's home, a registered landmark, then spend the evening across the river in Philadelphia. But as I crossed the bridge into Camden, a familiar anxiety came over me, the same anxiety a cop feels the first day he arrives at work in a lousy neighborhood. I didn't think there were many ghettos as bad as the West Side of Chicago, but Camden seemed pretty bad: groups of men standing on the corner, gang-banging for sure, a complete absence of commerce, empty buildings, many boarded up. I instinctively reached to the right side of my belt to feel for my pistol, but then I realized it wasn't with me. Cautiously I followed the directions of the GPS, until it announced I had arrived.

There, to my right, was the home Whitman lived in at the end of his life. He died on the second floor. My heart rate started picking up. I had been reading his poems since I was about nineteen years old, almost every day. At one point, I had memorized the first 150 lines of "Song of Myself," practicing each day as I walked home from work. Memories of first discovering his poetry flooded over me as I got out of the car. Whitman existed for me as the other side of an imaginative pole, the opposite of Kennedy's and García Márquez's magical realism. Whitman's poetry was all about the real world as it was, with none of the movement into the fantastical. There was also in his poetry a deep commitment and celebration of the American republic, of democracy, with none of the sympathy for the kind of revolution that the magical realists seemed to love.

I read every Whitman biography I could find, and, just before the trip, I had read about the years after he wrote the first edition of *Leaves of Grass*. The book did not sell as well as Whitman anticipated. It did not generate the public celebration he had been hoping for. But there was a darker force operating in his life beyond the desire for public approval and sales. In the years after he published the first edition of *Leaves*, Whitman fell into a deep depression, one that would not abate. There were many causes, no doubt, including the burden of being a homosexual in that era, and the unending problems and tragedies in his own family, but it was something even more deeply distressing than that. It struck me as odd that as Whitman published one of the masterworks in American literature, he would fall into that deep depression. Wouldn't he be euphoric that he finally found the voice he had been searching for?

As I walked up to the Whitman House, I felt a relief from my doubts about magical realism, my sense that there was something false, something profane in the magical side of it, particularly when I tried to apply it to Chicago. Here I entered the welcome world of Whitman's vital first-person "barbaric yawp." The political disparities between the two literary worlds again struck me, the fact, on the one hand, that Whitman's poetry was devoted to preserving the republic, even chronicling his work in the hospitals where the Civil War wounded ended up. And then, on the other, there was the connection to revolutionaries, Marxists, in the magical

realists, who fought to overthrow this republic. The distinc-
tions were not so easy. Whitman, for example, did not
support the abolitionists. He believed preserving the
republic was more important than abolishing slavery. What
about what the Marxists had done in the last century? And
what about the fact that I myself was a cop? My life needed a
sorting out, a clarification. Whitman was long gone, and the
magical realists were all the rage. I knocked, anyway.

Walt, it's me. Can you help me out?

No one answered. Knocked again. No answer. I scanned
up and down the block. This was no neighborhood to be
standing out front for thirty minutes. Had the caretaker left?
Would he come back? Had he blown me off? My heart sank,
much as it had in Albany. I looked around, up and down the
block. Knocked again. I was about to pull out my cell phone
and call the caretaker when I heard the sound of a creaking
old window open, and a middle-aged white guy, somewhat
burly like me, stuck his head out a window on the top floor.
His hair was messed up, and he looked frazzled. Had I interrupted his lunch, I wondered. Maybe there was a room
where caretakers could eat and hang up their coats, go
on break.

"Can I help you?" he said.

"Yes. I called earlier about getting a tour. I guess I'm a
little early," I said.

"Yes, you are. Can you give me a few minutes?"

"Sure. I'm sorry."

"Oh, it's no problem," he said unconvincingly.

There was a long silence, almost too long. Then, finally,
from where I was outside I could hear him walking down the

stairs and approaching the door. Again, as he opened the door, he looked frazzled. One of the buttons on his shirt was undone. Maybe he had been sleeping, I thought. The care-taker was friendly and invited me in, right into the front door of Walt Whitman's home. But he seemed flustered, nervous, as if he was trying to hide something. He kept looking me in the eye, trying to draw my attention. As he spoke, I heard a creaking sound off to my right, over his shoulder. I stole a glance in that direction and saw another man move quickly into the back area of the home, then out the back door. Now everything made sense. I had arrived early in the middle of the caretaker's afternoon rendezvous with a lover. He was nervous that I would figure it out. I played completely clue-less. Once the caretaker knew his lover was gone and all was safe, he relaxed and began giving me the tour.

What a thrill to walk into the home of a writer from a century earlier whom I had been reading my entire adult life. I sat in the parlor room where Whitman's guests waited until he was ready to see them. Then there was his bedroom on the second floor, windows overlooking the street. I remem-bered the image from several photos I'd seen in the various biographies I had read. There was the table he sat at and his chair, next to them the bed where he had died. Whitman had lived in hotels and rooming houses most of his life. It was only in the last stage of his life that he purchased this build-ing. He had suffered a series of strokes ever since his middle age, so he took in a widow who shared the building and acted as his housekeeper. In his later years, Whitman's work as a Civil War nurse was as important to him as the writing of his poems. Toward the end of his life, he often wrote letters to soldiers he had cared for during the war. I remembered that Aeschylus, the Greek tragic writer, wanted nothing about his writing life mentioned on his tombstone. Instead, he wanted it to say that he had fought in the great battles against the Persian invasion.

As I was leaving the house, the caretaker gave me directions to the cemetery nearby where Whitman was buried. I pulled my rental car onto the grounds, spotting a worker cutting the grass. "Whitman," I shouted over the roar of some machine. He pointed to one of the roads. "Follow it around," he said. After a long turn and a small hill, I saw Whitman's burial place. It was a mausoleum, gated off. Whitman had been buried there along with several family members. It was a grand structure, something Whitman designed and paid for. There was, to me, a bit of hubris in it, as if Whitman was giving himself some of the pomp he had not attained as a writer in his own lifetime. Whitman had written glowing reviews of his own poems under pseudonyms. Dishonesty? Yes. Narcissistic, sure. But Whitman believed in his poems unto his end. I smiled at it. Just inside the gates were pieces of paper, various poems, essays, messages left behind. Most of the missives seemed written by young people. I sat there for an hour or so, took some pictures, then headed into Philadelphia and turned in my rental car. I stayed the night, then early the next morning took a train to New York City, where I met two old friends for the weekend.

New York is an imposing city for a visiting writer. It asks you all the time if you can measure up, if you are worthy to wander a city where thousands of writers had lived and written there, including Whitman. This great duality tugging at me wouldn't go away: the magical realists and their affinity for revolution, on the one hand, Walt Whitman and the American democracy, his work to preserve the Union, on the other. I was tied to both of them. In my life I had moved between the two. The disparity between them suggested that some part of my life had been resting on something fraudulent. But first I had to find these forces working in Chicago itself, then clarify them. The quest held an appeal. Finding them, I could shine them up with the right words, make them glossy, and set them out for the world to see. One vision would have to win over the other, or I must find some way to merge the two, that or stand next to them with a stupid grin on my face for the rest of my witless life.

But I still had no idea, not the slightest clue, how to do it. And as I walked around New York City, I saw a few cops on the corners talking to one another. I remembered I was also a cop, a representative of the law, a job I had largely wandered into, and I had no idea if that job was bringing me closer to the task at hand or pushing me away.

Chapter 4

PROFILING

I was headed to Hyde Park again, this time in my car with a new manuscript. It was wrapped up in a rubber band on the seat next to me. I took Lake Shore Drive south because it was faster and because I wanted to see Lake Michigan as I drove. Today, I admitted to myself, likely marked the end of my tenuous legitimacy in the literary world. My first book had done well, garnering positive reviews from several national newspapers and magazines. It had also sold well. I had been interviewed on the radio and television. In the glow of this success, I had signed another contract with the University of Chicago Press, excited about the prospect of working on a new book, from start to finish, with Robert. Yet I had simmering doubts the entire time I worked on it. My first book was mostly about hauling dead bodies to the morgue. Now my dilemma about the revolution, the magical realists, and being a cop had intensified. This dilemma became the soil of my second book. In it, I had moved into key murder cases in which offenders convicted of the most heinous crimes had been released from prison, their advocates claiming they were wrongfully convicted. These advocates were revolutionaries or supporters of revolutionaries who battled the police in the infamous 1968 riots downtown. My second book chronicled my growing doubt about these wrongful conviction claims. As I moved more deeply into these cases, and the certainty that these men were truly guilty of the murders for which they had originally been convicted, I sensed I was also moving deeper into the magical, though a Chicago form of it. For what could be more magical than a convicted killer released and transformed into an innocent hero?

The core case was a double murder committed by gang member Anthony Porter in 1982. Porter was a notorious stick-up man and gang enforcer on the South Side in the projects that were nicknamed "the Hole." He frequented Washington Park, often hanging out in the bleachers next to a public pool. On a hot August night, Porter entered the pool area with a pistol. He was keyed up, with good reason. A few weeks earlier, he had shot a man in the head over a barking dog. Miraculously, the bullet went around the man's skull and exited the back. A warrant was issued for Porter's arrest. A week later, two police officers spotted him. As they approached, he raised a pistol and fired, then fled. The officers gave chase but lost him. With the warrant for shooting the man in the head, Porter's extended rap sheet, and the shots fired at the police, Porter certainly knew he was in for a long prison stint.

Late at night in the summer, residents often sneaked into

the pool for a swim. Tonight was no different. Two friends, Henry Williams and William Taylor, had arrived at the pool for a swim. Henry Williams had just gotten out of the pool when Porter approached. Williams's friend William Taylor was still swimming. As Porter approached Williams, he stuck a pistol in Williams's face and demanded his money. Williams only had two dollars. Porter took the two dollars and told Williams it was his lucky day. Porter then walked up into the bleachers. A short time later, Taylor got out of the pool. He heard gunshots, saw Porter standing over a couple, firing at them. Then Taylor saw Porter run out of the park right in front of him, Porter still carrying his pistol.

The male victim, Jerry Hillard, was shot in the head and fell to the bleacher floor. The female victim, Marilyn Green, was shot three times, the fatal bullet entering her neck then going down through her body. She was holding her neck as she stumbled down the bleachers. She waved down two police officers, pointing to Porter, but she could not speak. They stopped Porter but, finding no gun, they let him go. She stumbled out of the park to two other officers in the middle of a traffic stop. They put her into a squad car that took her to the hospital, where she died. Some detectives went to Hillard in the stands and heard him make snoring sounds. They knew from experience that he was dying, so they, along with the two witnesses who had encountered Porter just before he shot Green and Hillard—one who had been robbed and the other an eyewitness to the shooting—carried Hillard down the bleachers to a police wagon below. Hillard died.

The two witnesses were taken to the station. William Taylor, one of the eyewitnesses, didn't want to finger Porter

for fear of his life. He knew Porter's gang could harm his
family or him. But detectives Charles Salvatore and Dennis
Gray worked on him. They got some dinner and ate together.
Eventually Taylor came clean. Taylor told the detectives how
he saw Porter shoot the victims, how Porter then ran right by
Taylor with the pistol still in his hand. The detectives called
the state's attorney to get a warrant for Porter's arrest, what
would be his second warrant after shooting a man in the
head a few weeks earlier. The state's attorney arrived.
Nervous that the two witnesses had been drinking, he
declined to sign a warrant. The detectives were frustrated.
The prosecutor suggested all of them—the detectives, the
witnesses, and the prosecutor—go back to the park and walk
through the crime. The detectives agreed. It was now almost
a whole day since the shooting.

The witnesses walked the prosecutor and detectives
through the crime. Afterward, on the way back to the car,
Detective Gray spotted two men in the park. He decided to
approach them on the off chance they knew something
about the shooting. Gray suddenly called out to Salvatore
and the prosecutor. They approached. One of the men
admitted they had both witnessed the shooting. Their
description matched the account of the two other witnesses
already with the detectives, down to the smallest details,
including the fact that Marilyn Green was holding her neck
and what route she took out of the park. The detectives then
knew with a certainty rare in many murder cases that Porter
was their man. Porter turned himself in a few days later. He
was tried and sentenced to death, his long, extremely violent
history cited by the judge. Porter remained on death row as

his appeals wandered through the courts. Then, in 1998, Porter was within a few days of being executed when he was granted a stay based on the claim that his IQ was too low. Shortly afterward, a professor and students from Northwestern University's Innocence Project at the Medill School of Journalism got involved in the case. They suddenly announced that another man, Alstory Simon, had committed the murders.

The professor, David Protess, and his private investigator, Paul Ciolino, as well as several students taking a class at the Innocence Project, came forward with a bizarre videotaped confession from Alstory Simon. On the tape, Simon claimed he was the shooter, not Porter. He said that he had shot Hillard and Green over a drug dispute. With Simon's so-called "confession," Porter was released from death row and Simon arrested. Six months later, Simon confessed in court and was sentenced to thirty-seven years. But soon after Simon went to prison, he began claiming he was innocent, that he had been duped into confessing by Protess and Ciolino. Simon claimed he wasn't even in the park at the time of the murders. Furthermore, Simon's confession stood in stark contrast to the detectives' investigation. No witnesses had mentioned Simon at the crime scene, either by name or description. No witnesses afterward, nothing. Few people listened to Simon's retraction until I became involved in the case, along with a few other people, including a retired journalist, some lawyers, and two private investigators who were former federal agents. We pored over the immense number of documents in the case and saw clearly that Simon had nothing to do with the murders. More so, I tracked down the

original investigating detectives, who were accused of
framing Porter, and went through their investigation step by
step, bolstered by their reports. This process reinforced
Porter's guilt and Simon's innocence.

It would be difficult to overestimate the influence of the
Porter exoneration upon the Illinois criminal justice system
and the public imagination, the image of Porter emerging
from death row into the embracing arms of David Protess.
The case garnered international coverage, and the governor,
George Ryan, said he was so moved by the Porter exoneration
that he suspended the death penalty in Illinois. The Porter
exoneration gave life to what became known as the wrongful
conviction movement, the claim that dozens of other inmates
were wrongfully convicted. The movement spread beyond
Illinois. Soon universities were opening their own Innocence
Project departments. But as I researched first the Porter
exoneration, then others, and the possibility that I could
prove Porter guilty and Simon innocent, I began to see two
things: the bid to release so many convicted killers was part
of what I saw as a larger revolutionary movement taking
shape, and the true darkness within this revolution was what
the magical realists had always denied.

A few years after he pardoned Porter, Governor Ryan
pardoned several other inmates on death row. These exonerations were justified through the other great accomplishment of the wrongful conviction movement: the vilification
of a Chicago Police commander, Jon Burge, on the South
Side of Chicago. Relentlessly pushing the claim that Burge
and his men were torturing confessions out of suspects,
some innocent, some not, the claims were eventually used by

Ryan to justify several other key exonerations. The mythology of the police being racist torturers fulfilled the vilification of the police that first emerged after the 1968 riots at the Democratic Convention in Chicago. Indeed, the accusers of Burge and his men had strong ties to the most violent groups fighting with the police in 1968. The vilification of Burge and his men revealed that this battle had never truly ended in the city. It had only taken on new forms, moving from the streets to the courtrooms and newspaper rooms.

But just as the exoneration of Porter in 1999, and then the exonerations of more convicted men based upon their claims of abuse at the hands of Burge, signified a key victory for the revolutionaries from the 1960s, undermining the Porter exoneration and springing Alstory Simon from prison initiated my own battle against their established order, my own revolutionary life. This revolutionary life was fraught with danger, and the complexities often seemed too difficult to manage, but it was irresistible. My embracing of this counter-revolutionary life begged a question: Was I doing it for the thrill of attacking the newly established order, or because it was the right thing to do? These cases were not something one could get wrong, one could lie about, for Burge and his men were accused of the most heinous abuses.

Each time I turned in a new draft of a chapter of this second book to Robert, he praised it. He seemed as excited about the possibilities in the stories as I was. Yet I had a profound doubt that the book would ever see print at the University of

Chicago, and I repeated this to Robert every time we met. The reason was that the University of Chicago worked closely with Northwestern on wrongful conviction cases. Their law school, like Northwestern's, had been responsible for getting many of these accused killers out. Among university intellectuals, the advocates for these exonerations were unassailable heroes. I could not see the university publishing a book from a lowly patrolman telling them they were all wrong. There was a powerful arrogance among these lawyers and academics, the sense that they knew better than anyone —the detectives, the prosecutors, the judges, the appeals courts—what had happened in these murder cases. Moreover, these lawyers, activists, and academics based most of their claims of innocence on the argument that the police framed suspects. They pushed the narrative that the Chicago Police were racist torturers, even claiming that the detectives framed men they knew were innocent, often torturing them. Jon Burge remained their poster child. Activists had many of Burge's cases thrown out, and convicted men were set free. It was bizarre to see men like Anthony Porter walk out of the death row section of an Illinois prison, an entourage of students often surrounding them, greeting them like rock stars. Former inmates then sued the city, often making millions for themselves and their lawyers.

Eventually Burge himself was convicted, never of torture, but instead of perjury and obstruction of justice in written interrogatories about a wrongful conviction lawsuit. As I was driving that day to my first meeting at the press with an editor other than Robert, Burge was serving a four-year term in a federal penitentiary. With the conviction of Burge, it was now heresy for anyone in the city to question the claim that he was a racist torturer. For any cop to do so made that cop appear as if he were a pissed-off, jaded officer, unable to see beyond his own rage and bias. Nevertheless, Robert had seen clearly what I was doing as I wrote the book, and he had assured me he could get it published. Then, with a first draft completed, Robert called me up and told me he had accepted a job in Texas, and he would be leaving before my book was completed.

So now I was heading down to Hyde Park to meet an executive editor of the press, certain he would cut me loose. Without Robert, I had lost my most crucial supporter. And if the U of C Press dumped me, who else would pick me up? I imagined sending letters to agents, trying to speak with other publishers. It could take months, maybe even years. As I drove, I was torn between relief that I would finally know where I stood with the press and resentful and angry that they would, I anticipated, toss me aside because my book was so politically incorrect. As I drove, I told myself not to profile, not to make hasty conclusions about the people there. Keep an open mind. But if I were being honest with myself, there was a growing sense of loss for me as I perceived something slipping away, for I had fantasies of being known as a Chicago writer, being regularly published by one of its most prestigious institutions, the University of Chicago. I liked the idea of writing a new book every few years and sending it to the press, meeting with Robert regularly to review the manuscript, cover designs, and layouts. That was how I wanted to live my life, and my first book gave me entrance into that fantasy life. Now I feared it was likely going to end. With the closing of this door, I felt my life slipping back away from legitimacy into the subversive, like some kind of radical. As I pulled off at Fifty-Seventh Street and drove into Hyde Park, the buildings of the university campus, set as they were in Gothic quadrangles, heightened my feeling of alienation, for these ornate buildings housed some of the most revered intellectuals in the country, and they were about to shut their doors on me.

The editor who greeted me at a sandwich shop near the university looked every bit the university guy. He was wearing a tweed coat with patches on the elbows, glasses too, and was sporting a neatly trimmed beard, and right there I shamefully profiled him, immediately forgetting his real name and replacing it with one I liked better: Professor Tweed. I was wearing my usual sloppy T-shirt and jeans. As he stood up to shake hands, there was that nervous tension you sense when you are a cop, the uneasiness in people not used to being around police officers, the excessive politeness that you know may turn into a long-winded story about police violating the rights of their drunken brother-in-law or a ticket five years earlier on Lake Shore Drive. What a contrast to my initial meeting with Robert so many years ago. The editor's body movements were rigid and tight. In them, I sensed that he looked upon this meeting as an unpleasant obligation, and I knew right then he had made up his mind against publishing my book. Why would he want to publish it? After all, my book alleged grievous conduct at his school and other universities by academics just like him. I figured he probably felt guilty because I had done so well for his press with my first book. In me a writer's resentment welled up, the recollection of unpaid hours of toil, the loneliness of it, the many dead ends and furtive trips to interview someone, and the fact that I would be on my own again, publishing-wise, after I thought I had landed a prestigious local publisher for the rest of my career.

It dawned on me that the possibility of meeting another Robert in the publishing world was slight. But at the same time, I also felt a liberation. Robert had been a kind of buffer for me against guys like this editor. That is one reason we worked well together. Without him and his buffer, things would probably have not worked out for the first book. Part of me suddenly wanted very much to be away from the U of C Press. Back and forth I would go with these emotions at the lunch and in the months ahead, resentful at having lost a publisher, grateful not to have to deal with them without Robert.

Waiters generally dread lunch shifts. Usually, they have to work lunches until they prove themselves and some evening shifts open up. To make any money on lunches, they have to turn the tables in the brief one-hour lunch rush, meaning they have to seat each table twice in the narrow span of an hour, a difficult thing to do. Everyone comes in at once. The entrées cost less so the checks are smaller. Smaller checks, smaller tips. People have to return to work, so they want what they want right away. In a restaurant that caters to the university crowd, there is also the risk that a teacher/student might come in and spend several hours going over some topic as they slowly eat their lunch or, in our case, an editor and a writer. Sitting down at the table, I caught the disappointed glance of the waitress when she saw my manuscript placed on the table by Tweed. She was a young African American woman, a student, I figured, or a bohemian type from the way she was dressed. Maybe both.

Tweed did not pick up on her disappointment. I doubted he had ever waited tables. But, as a longtime service worker, I took note of her frustration. When she came to the table, Tweed hit her with several questions about the menu, oblivious to the fact that all her other tables had just been seated as well and they all wanted her attention. His questions took a long time, with pauses as his finger went across the menu. It was a sandwich shop, for Christ's sake, I thought. She stood waiting for him to finish his questions. After he grilled her on the menu, he relaxed in his chair and tried to make small talk with her about how he liked corned beef or turkey. I saw her pen twitching. She was getting angry. I couldn't blame her. Asking about the menu was one thing. What came next was another.

"Have you been working here a long time?" Tweed asked, sitting back. *Robert*, I thought, *where the fuck are you and why did you go to Texas?* It seemed to me Tweed, in his nervousness over our meeting, was putting on a kind of performance for me, trying, perhaps, to show me he could relate to a blue-collar worker.

I could see the waitress's eyes narrow, slicing through

him, thinking, *What the fuck is it to you how long I've worked here, motherfucker? What the fuck kind of sandwich do you want?*

"Not long," she said coldly.

"Wow, looks like you're getting swamped. I'll have the turkey sandwich and some coffee," I said, pushing things along.

Each time she came back to the table, Tweed had some new observation to make, some question to pose to her. Each time she bristled, as did I.

Tweed treated me with the same arrogance. He knew I wanted to know desperately whether the press would proceed with the book and, if so, under what terms. He knew how desperate is the life of a writer. This was something I detested about being a writer, the power publishers and editors have over you. But he waited. He asked me personal questions, stuff about my background, where I worked. People often probe you when you are cop, like you are a monkey at the zoo, and I felt this in his questions. The questioner is waiting for you to say or do something that will reveal some inner bias or anger in you, or just some secret. First they probe, then they poke. I deflected the questions. Then Tweed got into the specific criminal cases in my book, grilling me in detail about every aspect of the argument I was making about the Porter murders. I began to sense that the intent behind the questions was also to probe me for some weakness, to undermine my argument, probably for him to find some justification to reject the manuscript. I sensed he knew deep down that the rejection to come was unjustified, that he was tossing me by the wayside even after the success of my first book, the contract for the second, and the fact that

Robert had told everyone he was excited about the second as
well. Clearly, by his questions, he had read the manuscript
thoroughly. But the conversation was more of an interrogation, another sign that he was going to reject the manuscript.
As I sat across from Tweed, who was formulating another
angle of attack about my claims on a double homicide in
1982, I decided this entire relationship was hopeless. I
couldn't imagine the long, difficult, frustrating process of
editing a book with this guy. He was nothing like Robert. But
I resented the interrogation all the same. It was one thing to
reject a manuscript, but another to put someone through this
grilling before doing so. I had done well for the press, I
thought. Now I was being grilled by this guy.

"There, to me," I heard Tweed say, "is the problem with
your argument, the fact that the witness recanted."

I looked up at him, smiling triumphantly, as if he felt he
finally had found the fatal logical flaw in my book. I stared at
him, his words still ringing in my mind, and I considered
them. He was all wrong. He missed the central point. Detectives in the 1982 murder investigation had found two groups
of witnesses a day apart, who both provided identical statements about Porter being at the crime scene and committing
the murders, independent statements that proved conclu-
sively that Porter was the killer. Northwestern investigators
had never resolved the discovery of independent witnesses,
which confirmed the validity of all their statements. I had
had enough of this guy.

"You're missing the point," I said, his smile fading. "The
detectives in that case discovered two groups of witnesses at
different times, witnesses who had no opportunity to

converse with each other because the first group had been at the police district since moments after the murder. The second group of witnesses was found the following day in the park. So how could their identical statements about the murders, down to the smallest details, how could they be false or coerced? What are the chances that both groups would say the offender shot with his left hand, that one of the victims fell, rose up holding her neck, and walked out the north end of the park, if either group were lying or if the police were coercing a false statement?"

There was a silence. His smile waned. I could see his mind spinning. I wanted to go home, wanted to get away from these ivory towers. What the hell was I thinking? Robert was an anomaly as an editor, a great stroke of luck for me, but now he was gone. I let the silence grow, staring at him. It's an old police trick. Just pause and stare at the person, and they will begin talking nervously. Tweed grew uncomfortable, fidgeted. He looked away from me.

"Well, there are some problems with the manuscript," he said, "narrative problems."

"I'm sure there are. It's only a draft. That is something Robert and I would normally iron out together," I said, thinking what manuscript doesn't have some narrative problems?

Another silence.

"Well," he said, leaning back in his chair. "It's a potential masterpiece, but I'm not going to publish it."

"It is?"

I didn't see that coming.

"Yes, it is."

"Then why aren't you going to publish it?"

"Because I could never get the board to agree to publish what you are saying about Jon Burge."

Well, I thought, *at least he is now being honest.*

"What about the ivory towers and free speech and all that, differing points of view?"

"It's just not going to happen. They won't do it."

I stared at him. I was crazy to think that the University of Chicago would publish my book. It was stupid of me even to come to this lunch. And to have to endure the two hours' questioning by Tweed added to my humiliation. I couldn't stand Tweed anymore, couldn't watch him torture this poor waitress again. It was my day off. Robert and I almost always had two-hour lunches, talking literature and writing. The time just flew by.

The restaurant was now mostly empty. I saw the waitress lingering in the corner, sneaking a sip of coffee. No doubt she wanted to go home, but she had to wait for us. I gathered some things on the table to let Tweed know it was time to go. As we rose up, he was talking about helping me get an agent.

Whatever, I thought.

I let him walk out first so I could steal a glance at the check. Sure enough, he had put a ten percent tip down, oblivious to the fact that we had tied up the table for the waitress's whole shift. I reached into my pocket and grabbed a tenner, sneaked it on top of the check, and followed him out.

Chapter 5

COVERT

I stand up from my desk at police headquarters and announce to my sergeant I have to get something from my car. He keeps his eyes on the screen and nods okay after a pause that is one beat too many. These forays of mine to the parking lot are becoming too frequent, and I know he is getting suspicious. There is something rebellious about me he can't quite finger, but he doesn't like it.

Outside it is chilly. The ground is wet from an earlier rain. My little Ford Focus is in the far corner, near the el tracks. It is late afternoon, so the parking lot is half-empty. I can see my car is parked by itself, alone. Pulling up the hood of my jacket, I look around to see if anyone is near me, if anyone is following. I glance up at the building to see if anyone is watching me from a window. I walk through the rows of the parking lot, keeping my head down. My old partner and academy classmate, Shannon, is meeting me. She is sneaking over from the adjacent Ninth District in between calls for police service. If she gets an assignment on the radio, we can't meet. We'd have to try again later and, doing so, I'd risk pushing it too far with my sergeant by asking to go outside again. I scan the parking lot to see if Shannon is already waiting, then glance at my cell phone to see if she has sent a message.

Nothing.

I glance into the front of my car from my seat on the back bumper. It's a mess—wrappers from cafés and fast-food restaurants litter the floor. Residue from muffins and scones remains on the seats. There were old towels and rags, coffee cups, books, and articles inches deep on the floor and seats. Neither of my windows rolls down anymore, so there is a musty scent. The air conditioner is broken. I baked in the car during the summer. The car needs new brakes, and the maintenance lights on the dashboard no longer work. I have to check the tires every few days and fill them up. It is time for a new car, I figure. It is nice to have a job where I can afford to go out and buy a new car on credit. The police job affords such middle-class luxuries, a condo, vacations, pension. Before becoming a cop, I had struggled in the service industry for more than a decade, working as a door-man. In the hotel business, I was just getting by, though the work was exhausting. I like the comfort and security of the police department.

At my car, I open the hatchback. I pull copies of my new book, *Crooked City*, out of the box one at a time, set them on another box as a makeshift desk, open the front cover, then take the dark marking pen from my shirt pocket and sign the bottom of the title page inside the front cover. I repeat this fifteen times, stacking the signed copies in the corner. I love the way they looked stacked, one facing one way, the next, the other. When I am done, I put them into another smaller box and look for Shannon's car. Just then my phone alerts me I have a text message.

"Where are you?" it says.

"Far corner, by the el tracks," I type.

"Okay, OTW."

"Niner Five, Red Dog out," I type, smiling. Shannon hates when I type this fake police jargon on messages or say it on the phone, so I do it all the time.

I look at the entrance to the lot. There is a squad car pulling past the gate. It slowly moves my way. Shannon is technically out of her district, but only by a few blocks. Still, she could get jammed up for doing this. You're not supposed to leave your district. The cars have tracking devices in them now. As she pulls up, the rear hatch to her SUV pops open. I go around back, carrying the box of books, and set it down there, then walk around to her side.

Shannon, like Robert, is from the enclave of Irish on the far South Side, Mount Greenwood, a neighborhood filled with cops, firemen, and other city workers. After the academy, we were partners together in the Fifth District. She had become one of my best friends on the job. When I was out with back surgery, stuck in the hospital for eight days in intense pain, she traveled from the South Side every day to visit. She was a nurse before she was a cop, and she double-checked the care I was getting in the hospital, talking to the nurses about what I needed. I was so doped up, I didn't even know what day it was. She came the day I was released and drove me to a friend's house in Oak Park. Now she was joining in this clandestine operation to sell my book to cops all over the city. It struck me once again how my police friends were among the best friends I had ever had. As I walk to the passenger side, her window rolls down.

"There are fifteen in there. You sell them for fifteen bucks and keep five. I get ten," I say.

"I'm not taking any money. I'll give you all fifteen," she says in an assertive South Side voice, letting me know any further argument is pointless.

I will have to buy her some present instead, so I let the subject go for now.

Her partner is sitting in the passenger side, a little baffled by what is going on.

"This is Marty, my old partner from Five," Shannon says to her.

"You guys worked in Five together?" the partner asks.

"Well, not really worked together necessarily. It was more like I was Marty's training officer," Shannon says.

This claim is our oldest and most frequent form of harassing each other. We started the job at the same time, but we always bait each other by claiming we were the training officer, especially to other cops. Shannon's partner laughs.

"Yeah," I say to Shannon's partner. "You probably don't know this yet, but you should if you are working with Shannon. You see, Shannon suffers from a disorder called DPS. Have you ever heard of it?"

The partner, laughing again, shakes her head.

"It's called Delusional Police Syndrome. She recalls

things exactly the opposite of how they actually were. You see, not only did I train her, but I failed her twice. It was only our friendship and her political connections on the South Side that compelled me to pass her the third time. Did I make the right call? I just don't know. I go back and forth with it," I say, waving my hand back and forth. "But at this point, it's water under the bridge."

"We can go right upstairs and get the performance evaluations if you want," Shannon says, pointing at headquarters. We keep the argument going for a few more minutes before Shannon changes the subject and tells me the books are selling in the Ninth District, that people like it. A call comes over the radio, a gang disturbance, and she has to go.

I'm alone in the far corner of the parking lot. It's overcast, and a light sprinkle has begun. The rear hatch door is still open and gives me cover. Boxes half-filled with books are scattered in the back of my car. A northbound train approaches above me, sparks flying where the wheels meet the tracks, throwing up an intense blue light. The sparks fall to the ground below. I should be getting back to my job. My coworkers and supervisors are waiting for me on the fourth floor, but I like the rain, the rattling trains above, and the skyline. I can see Comerica Park.

I pull one of the boxes toward myself. I reach into my pocket for my key chain and use a key to rip the seal on the box, then open the flaps, revealing four neat stacks of my book *Crooked City*. The book chronicles my investigation into several key wrongful conviction cases, investigations that concluded these exonerations were frauds. I look at the books stacked in two separate piles in the box. My mind goes back over the cases I had been looking at for more than five years, in particular the 1999 Anthony Porter exoneration. Part of the narrative that got the offenders like Porter released from prison was the deep suspicion people held about the police, particularly in Chicago. People believed there was a deep racism, violence, and ignorance that compelled officers to frame innocent men. The public believed that officers looked the other way from the crimes being committed by corrupt officers, what the media called "the blue code of silence." There was a time in my life when I would have wholeheartedly believed such claims, particularly when I was a college student.

I no longer believed these exonerations were true. Instead, I began to see a family of murder cases in 1982 that all culminated in what I believed was the release of truly guilty men. The stories became a vehicle in which I might document my own changing worldview in the city, from then until now. The exonerations, therefore, offered themselves as something more than legal history or even opinion. They became, to me, allegories, upon which I hoped I might become one of those rare writers who understands his own time and his own place in it. Yet the deeper I went into these murders, the more I was cast out from the official world of publishing, from a whole world of legitimacy. The fate of the detectives in these cases seemed prophetic of my own writing career. Many of them had been ruined, their names in the paper every day, accused of the worst crimes. Jon Burge was in prison. I feared ending up like the detectives, vilified, humiliated. Look at me in the parking lot. But how could I stop, knowing that these cases, like Anthony Porter's exoneration, were false? Just as much, how could I ignore the possibility of finally putting my own narrative stamp on Chicago's corruption by writing about these cases?

With this second book, I have, without being formally aware of it, entered the city's conspiratorial life. The city's corruption is such that every endeavor is blunted into crime, then every ambition into conspiracy. The rules that govern these conspiracies are the city's native laws, and it is meaningless and dangerous to live in ignorance of them. I had, for too long—one reason, I decided, that my life was filled with movements lacking direction or logic. My movements were now furtive, but they at least held some purpose, however foolish or absurd, and I am grateful for it. I couldn't help but think I had moved toward this condition from some deep instinct. My own rebelliousness, my own antipathy to the way the world was, came alive in my mind, a clear record of my own affinity for the conspiratorial. All conspiracy is aimed at overthrowing something. Chicago, with its endless plots, seems to me a city given to revolution, for it harbors constantly the seeds of some takeover in one form or another.

I am moving into the revolutionary's dream, and I like it. I like how it gives purpose and hope, and that it is thrilling. Most of all, I like how it requires an imaginative life far more intense than anything mislabeled legitimate in the city. I look at myself in the parking lot with the hatch open, boxes of books all around me. The mantra of the revolutionary, the thing that keeps him going, is the belief that even as he moves downward, he is actually moving closer to his goal. He and his kind have been cast out from the farthest reaches of

power and legitimacy. The power of the revolution, the glory
of it, is that one can traverse the vast distances and obstacles
between the land of the outcast, like the one where I
currently reside in this parking lot, to the very pinnacle of . . .
of . . . *of what*, I ask myself. I neither knew the nature of my
counterrevolution nor its purpose, save for the fact that
wandering the city's crimes, particularly its murders,
revealed its revolutionary muse and, perhaps, mine.

With this in mind, I stand up, close the hatch of my car,
and walk slowly back to headquarters, my eyes darting back
and forth.

Chapter 6

INTERLUDE

A wave had pushed my body onto the rocks near Loyola, around the same time the sun broke across the eastern horizon, warming my body and drying off whatever clothes I was wearing, if any. It was the damnedest thing. I could see so much of what was taking place around me, but I couldn't see myself, my own image. I couldn't turn my head to look down and see what I was wearing. Nor could I look at my body for signs of how I had died or for how long I had been dead. How emaciated was I? How bad did I stink?

The sun hastened my rotting. That was a striking difference between the living and the dead. The living liked to gather in front of the sun and bask in it. The dead move away from it, first by being put in refrigerators, then, eventually, in the ground. There was also a striking difference between the water and the land. It was better to be dead in the water, where your degeneration is less offensive, since the water slowly erodes you and spreads your rotting out. The water

covers up much of your stench and filth, save from some
unlucky swimmer or water skier who happens upon you. On
land, you rot more quickly, and everyone sees it. People come
and stare at you, often people who knew you. A lot of times
they stand around, nodding their heads, as if your termina-
tion makes perfect sense. It's a kind of "I told you so"
nodding. They start whispering their interpretation to other
people, who also nod their heads. There's nothing you can
say to refute them. When you are in the water, people can
only stand on the shore and wonder about you in a kind of
reverie that is more gentle and understanding, more poetic
than someone who dies taking a shit or walks absently into
the path of a bus on the street or who ignominiously washes
up on the shore of a city they hated, but remained there
nevertheless, solely for a pension.

This duality between sun and dark, land and water,
reverberated through my own existence. I recalled that as a
writer I spent many a sunny day inside my ground-level
condo, working away in sweatpants. In the mornings, after
writing about murders, I was unshowered; my breath stank
from coffee and not brushing my teeth. Then I would take a
long shower, washing away my filth, brush my teeth, put on
relatively clean underwear, and emerge into the living world.
I would often come out in the afternoons to a blinding sunny
day, squinting with the sun on me. The parallels of my
writing life to the world of the dead strengthened my conviction that writing, that art in general, in its most elemental
form, is a religious undertaking, a way of squaring one world
with the other. In light of this, I wondered, what was the
meaning of my returning to Chicago as a corpse? For years I

had been trying to nail down the specific facts of murders, particularly who committed them, but now the circumstances of my death burdened me. Perhaps my corpse was now a key piece of evidence in the stories I had been writing about. Perhaps something could be gleaned from me that would prove much of what I had been saying about the wrongful conviction movement was true. Perhaps, on the other hand, I had amounted to nothing more than a mere nuisance, and in some ignominious way the city muses had done me in and tossed me into Lake Michigan. If so, why was I now being called back?

It was about this time I heard the voices of two young women approaching me on the paved path along the lakefront, right near Loyola University. I could make out clearly in my keen dead vision that they were students because they were carrying books, obviously on their way to an early class. They were chatting in a lively manner. As they approached, I reflexively tried to reach up and push my hair down to make myself more presentable, forgetting that I was dead and unable to move my arms, forgetting also that it was impossible to make a dead person presentable under any circumstances. I also found myself trying to call out to them, for whatever was in store for me, I wanted to get on with it, rather than bake in the sun all day. But I didn't know exactly what to say. It didn't matter. I couldn't shout anyway. After a few moments, I realized that the only thing that could notify them I was around was my stench. Well I knew from hauling dead bodies to the morgue that the smell, if the body was in an advanced state of decay, would carry for blocks and no one could ignore it. As if in answer to my thoughts, I heard the release of some gas from my body, and I knew the cloud of stench could very well reach them. There was a pause. Then it came.

"Oh my God. That is so disgusting. What is that?" said one of the girls, raising her hand to her face as if to block it.

I've never had a way with women, I said to myself.

"I don't know. Something is dead. I'm sure."

I heard more gas releasing from a lower extremity. What timing.

"Do you think it's a squirrel or a seagull?" asked one girl.

"No way. It has to be something larger," said the other.

"Well, what do we do?"

"Let's take a look."

"No way."

"C'mon. We'll just cross over the first rocks and look down there."

I heard their dainty sandals stepping lightly and cautiously on the rocks above me. I remembered that when my book about the Porter case had come out, I had tried to get some engagements at universities to tell the students my stories. A few departments had invited me, but most ignored me. This recollection intensified a familiar loneliness, one now alive even in my dead state. Then it came, a shriek comprised of two voices.

"Oh my God. It's a dead body," one girl said.

"His skin looks like he burned to death," said the other.

I had my first clue; I had likely been trapped and died in some city fire. The confirmation by one of the girls focused my memory, allowing me while resting on the rocks, stinking to all hell, to pore over the events that may have led to my demise in this burning. And so I became reflective in the period between the girls fleeing and the inevitable arrival of the Chicago Fire Department, along with whatever beat car showed up. Likely I would know the cops, since I had worked this neighborhood. It struck me once again how clearly the dead think. For if I had been able to focus on a theme while I was living the way I did lying dead on those rocks, I could have been a ten times better writer, because shit just flies through your dead mind without any distraction whatsoever. And I just let it do so, kind of like brainstorming in a way, until the seminal events settled themselves among all the images, something that would have taken years when I was living.

You know, I thought, *a guy could get used to this whole dead thing.*

Chapter 7

HAYMARKET

I t was a summer day and I was driving south on I-55, just off Lake Shore Drive. Next to me on the passenger seat was a bag containing my gas mask, helmet, and wooden stick. The gas mask was wrapped in its original plastic. I had worn it only once, during training. I looked at the straps hanging from it, trying to remember how you put it on and got it working. There was something you had to twist, I recalled, so I fumbled with the plastic container, hoping that part would reveal itself. How had I ended up working a job that required such equipment, I wondered. How had my life come to this day?

An image, a memory, came to me, intensifying the question. It was decades earlier, when I was at a Great Books college in Santa Fe, New Mexico, high in the mountains. The reading list was ominous at this school. Often you had to read two hundred pages a day of original work by some great thinker. I was struggling to keep up. Despite the workload, I spied a book in the bookstore that caught my eye, Karl Marx's famous collection of essays outlining the ideas behind communism, called the *Economic and Philosophic Manuscripts of 1844*. In these notes, published after he died, Marx was setting out his ideas about economics, alienation, and German philosophy. I was already starting to sense that my life would be doomed to blue-collar service industry jobs, like in restaurants and hotels, so I picked up the book and began reading. Marx was a seductive writer; his conception of man as doubly alienated in capitalism, its dehumanizing forces, was electrifying for me. I was supposed to be reading Plato and Aristotle, but more and more each day I found myself sneaking these manuscripts into the school café and wasting away an afternoon reading them, absorbed in the notion that all human history was working toward one grand climax, when the workers took over the world and everybody would be happy. Busboy one day, fully humanized the next.

Now I was on the other side of Marx's revolution, sipping the cup of drive-through coffee I'd just bought and eyeing the bagged pastry that would be my breakfast, driving on Lake Shore Drive with riot equipment, a pistol, and police uniform. I was a defender of private-property, free-market democracy. A few days earlier, several youths were caught in the midst of making firebombs, called Molotov cocktails, which, investigators said, the youths planned on hurling at the police during demonstrations for the NATO summit in the city. The discovery of these would-be bombers raised the tension in the city. Everyone was nervous, and many journalists harkened back to the 1968 riots during the Democratic National Convention. Would the police be out of control

again, many of them asked. Would we be out of control, I
wondered. Firebombs? The question rang in my mind
because I had been talking to many cops who had worked
the riots in 1968. Rather than portraying the cops as vigi-
lantes out to attack the demonstrators, most of them said
how nervous they were, nervous because there were so many
groups in the city out to get the cops, like the Black Panthers
and the more radical elements of the anti-war protesters.
Many of these groups were ranting about "killing the pigs."

My stomach fluttered at the notion of Molotov cocktails. I
imagined someone emerging from the demonstrators,
hurling an incendiary bomb at the police, and it exploding in
a large fireball around them. I had seen people die from
gunshots, stabbings, and car crashes. I had seen a woman
dragged from a burning building, her flesh tearing from her
bones, but I had never seen anyone intentionally set on fire,
being burned alive. How many people would be engulfed?
Would I see a coworker burned on the ground? Would some
officers end up in the burn unit? Then I thought about the
youthful offenders who had been caught making the bombs.
Were they so well organized that they had alibis figured out
ahead of time? Were there other demonstrators in the crowd
who would be false witnesses for them? What would it be
like to be severely burned and then see the offenders walk
away, unconvicted, the way the detectives in the Porter case
saw Porter walk free from his double murder? As I got closer
to headquarters, my heart was beating faster. This anxiety is
probably what the cops felt like all during the convention in
1968, only much worse. What kind of day was ahead?

My job that day was to monitor the demonstrations from

the fifth floor of headquarters, watching numerous high-definition televisions broadcasting images throughout the downtown area. I would try to spot any youth reaching into a backpack and pulling out a bomb. What if I missed it, I wondered. Even if I saw something, how could I get word out to the police on the street in time to warn them? I had no idea. It would be tough if we missed something that could prevent an attack. It also bothered me that I would be working inside. Only if the demonstrations got totally out of hand would I be called from headquarters to work on the street. I felt ashamed to be inside an air-conditioned building while most every other cop was working throughout the day and night in the summer heat, wearing all kinds of equipment. The demonstrators, mostly screaming youths, would be cursing them, throwing things at them, accusing them of every kind of evil for hours on end. Probably the police would be spit on.

What was also troubling about the emergence of the bombers was how it coincided with my second book, the one chronicling my growing doubt about offenders who had been released from prison on the claim that they were wrongfully convicted. At the time of the demonstrations, Alstory Simon was still in prison, languishing under the confession he had made to the murders after being coerced, he claimed, by Northwestern investigators. The demonstrations coincided with my book, and the attorneys who stepped forward to represent the accused bombers had become familiar to me as I investigated and wrote about the Anthony Porter exoneration. These attorneys harkened back to the late 1960s when the anti-war demonstrators turned violent, and later became colleagues and allies of David Protess at Northwestern University in the wrongful conviction movement. One of the law firms representing the would-be bombers was the People's Law Office (PLO), a firm that had formed in the wake of the battles between the police and the Black Panther movement in the late '60s and '70s. The PLO had moved steadily into defending other violent radical groups from that time onward, often basing their claims on police corruption. Eventually, in the 1980s, they spearheaded the movement against Chicago Police commander Jon Burge, claiming he was a racist torturer.

One group the PLO had worked closely with was the Weather Underground, or the Weathermen. A key member of the group was a woman named Bernardine Dohrn, who was eventually placed on the FBI's Most Wanted list for her role in several of the group's bombings. In the higher reaches of law enforcement and the criminal justice system, a debate raged about how to investigate the Weather Underground and other violent political groups. The FBI eventually determined that the Weather Underground was not just a criminal organization, it was a revolutionary group aimed at overthrowing the government. The magnitude of the group's violence, their radical Marxist literature, and their association with communist leaders compelled many in federal law enforcement to treat them as enemies of the state. Therefore, the FBI employed methods that violated constitutional rights, tactics like illegal wiretaps and stealing mail. It was these unconstitutional acts that allowed Dohrn to beat the criminal charges against her, successfully alleging that the FBI violated her rights in the course of their investigation. It was one of the earliest examples of these activists turning the tables on law enforcement, just as they would years later against the Chicago Police Department. After Dohrn beat the charges, she and her husband, Bill Ayers, moved into the mainstream. Both became college professors, Dohrn ultimately taking a job at Northwestern University. It was one of those magical transformations from depraved criminal to legitimacy, even though Dohrn's own mantra in the late 1960s and '70s was to initiate a revolution by "killing the pigs."

Of which I now was one.

Many of the former 1960s radical groups like the Black Panthers and the Weather Underground openly called themselves Marxists. They even visited communist countries in the 1970s and discussed revolutionary strategies with leaders there. As I drove to work and thought about what these activists eventually became—middle-class kids so turned on by the notion of revolution that they actually went to communist countries and met with their leaders, and then became terrorists of their own country—this hit a nerve for me. I recalled reading Marx in college, how seduced I had been. Then I looked at myself in my car, partially wearing my police uniform, riot gear and stick next to me. I was a person who dreadfully misapprehended his own world, either back then or now. In either case, I was coming to believe that much of my life had been a lie.

As soon as the youths accused of plotting a firebombing were apprehended, the PLO immediately engaged the legal strategy that they and Protess had employed for more than two decades: they claimed the police set up the would-be bombers. Since I had been reading so much about wrongful conviction cases, I immediately recognized the tactic. The narrative by the Northwestern investigators who freed Porter was that the Chicago Police were so evil they didn't care who really murdered the victims Marilyn Green and Jerry Hillard. The detectives, they argued, just decided the afternoon following the murders to pin the gruesome killings on Porter, even though the detectives knew he was innocent. They made the same argument against Burge and his men, unraveling one case after another. This was, in fact, the logic of the entire wrongful conviction movement.

As I pulled off Lake Shore Drive onto Thirty-Fifth Street, I recalled my infatuation with Marx's arguments. At that time, I would have bought the police frame-up theory in both the Porter and NATO cases. They were arguments championed by academics, who, at that time, had a powerful hold on my imagination, as if what they said was more official, more legitimate than what anyone else believed. Back then, I would have assumed that they had done the research and they operated with the utmost concern for getting the facts straight. Things were different now as I drove to work. My mind was crowded with the imagery of murder cases in which the killers were set free. I had become so familiar with these murders, I could replay them in my mind in great detail. I went back to the Porter murders in 1982.

Porter shot Hillard and Green in a crowded park. So many cops had responded to the scene. The radio lit up with "person shot" calls. All the cops knew the park and knew it was crowded because earlier that day an annual parade had been held there to celebrate the return to school. When the cops heard the call, they knew it could be anything, including a gang shoot-out. They knew there were likely numerous witnesses. Given all this activity all around the park, with so many cops involved and so many potential witnesses, how could the detectives who got the case later on that day concoct a story framing Porter? How could they be certain that so many cops already aware of what happened wouldn't front them out for framing Porter? How could they be certain another witness would not come forward and prove their account was false? Then where would the detectives be? Well, they'd be facing prison. But nonetheless this theory of the police framing Porter had become an official narrative.

By the time I was driving to work for the NATO demonstrations, I knew the detectives in the Porter case didn't frame anyone. I knew Porter was the shooter. I became certain of this after tracking down the detectives and hearing the account of their investigation. The narrative of their investigation disproved any allegation of misconduct and bolstered Porter's guilt beyond any doubt. It was easy for the jury to convict him. The narrative of the detectives' investigation, garnered from their reports and from long interviews on the phone and in diners, became a liberating process, not simply because these detectives would tell me things they would not tell anyone else. Wrongful conviction cases, including the Porter exoneration, were mired down in legal proceedings, depositions, trials, and evidence gathering, all going back decades. There was so much complexity that it was almost impossible to tell someone about the case without confusing them. It took days to lay it all out, and left one in a kind of opaque world of secondary sources. But the detectives' point of view, their investigation, imposed a clarity on the murders and the exonerations.

In these interviews with the detectives, there was usually one fact of the investigation that cut right through the entire case and simplified it. Detective Charles Salvatore, the lead detective in the Porter murders, delivered one such fact to me at our first meeting, the very story that I'd used to defend the soundness of the argument in my second book to Tweed a few days earlier, of how detectives discovered the second set of witnesses the day after the murders, witnesses who provided a detailed narrative of the shooting that matched the account of witnesses discovered at the crime scene. The matching witness accounts confirmed what had happened that night, for the second group did not know the first and they had no opportunity to speak to one another. It would therefore be virtually impossible for them both to be lying or to be wrong about what happened.

Salvatore's investigation proved rock solid. Incredibly, Protess and all the Northwestern students involved in the Porter case admitted under oath that they had never even bothered to speak to this second group of witnesses. They just ignored them and ran with the false narrative that the detectives had framed Porter. They also never bothered to contact the detectives. This central fact of independent witnesses discovered at different times, witnesses who did not know one another, providing identical statements,

undermined the entire theory by the Northwestern Innocence Project. But it didn't matter, in the end. Porter was still
cut loose and Alstory Simon was sent to prison. The detectives' investigation was necessarily obliterated from the
narrative of the case, the only way Porter could have been set
free from death row.

Now the same claims of the police framing offenders took
shape with the NATO bombers three decades later, during
my own career. The theory this time was that a collection of
officers would suddenly get together, construct an elaborate
trap of framing youths for making bombs at a time the whole
world was watching the city closely, the police in particular.
The most basic questions were never asked or answered.
How did these crooked cops form this plot? How did they get
supervisors to go along with it? How did they get warrants?
How did they know that all the officers would be willing to
stick to their frame-up, a frame-up that could get them all
years in prison, the loss of their jobs, if it were exposed?
What purpose would it serve? How would locking up these
youths on false charges benefit the cops or anyone? What
was the purpose behind it?

I pulled into the parking lot of police headquarters. As I got
out, I grabbed the cup of coffee and bagged pastry in one
hand, my police equipment in the other. It was a gorgeous
summer morning. The trees on the southwest section were
blooming. I always parked here because these trees blocked

the view from the windows at headquarters. I liked cutting across a far section of the lot by traversing the grass in this corner, walking amid the trees, and feeling the soft soil underneath my feet. I walked on it now, thinking how nice it would be to sit down in the grass for a while, strum my guitar if I had it with me. Even just taking off my shoes and walking barefoot would be nice. But how would that look, some cop half-dressed in his uniform, strumming a guitar next to the police parking lot on the day they were looking out for fire-bombers? Nevertheless, I looked around to see if anyone was watching. They weren't, so I stopped and sniffed some of the blossoms on the trees, reached up and pulled some off their stems. They were soft, like velvet. I should know what kind of trees these were, the way I knew the gang factions on the West Side, but I didn't. I rubbed some of the blossoms softly in my fingers for a minute, then put them in my pocket.

As I walked off the grass under the trees and back onto the pavement of the parking lot, I felt the melding of doom and possibility so peculiar to the city. In writing about the Anthony Porter exoneration, I had merged the detectives' method with my own literary ambition, concluding that it was the detectives' perspective that would finally offer up the right words in the right order. It was amazing where the detectives' perspective could take me, to any place a writer about the city needed to go. This perspective also moved to the edge of the other world, for I followed Detective Salvatore's investigation of the Porter murders to a place where I imagined better than ever before what it would be like to be murdered the way Marilyn Green was killed, facing your killer only a few feet away, seeing the gun and that menacing, crazy sociopath's glare behind it, the muzzle flash, and then to watch from some unknowable place the offender eventually walk free from prison, ecstatic, declared innocent, and celebrated as a victim and a hero, and to understand clearly from that unknowable place that Porter did it, that he fucking did it, that no-good motherfucker did it, and he was walking free as a hero in the most crooked city. Here was the imagery of Chicago's corruption. I knew before I could articulate it that in my meetings with Salvatore on the near West Side, where he broke down step by step his investigation of the case, I had found something utterly valuable, and I wouldn't leave it for a long time.

Halfway across the parking lot, I spied the Haymarket Memorial near the back entrance, where the cops enter headquarters. Instinctively I walked toward it. The memorial had moved in and out of my life at crucial times. Now it moved in again, guarding the rear door of police headquarters. I walked past it several times a day. We all did. In my growing intimacy with it, I began to call the memorial "Hay," short for Haymarket. Hay stands atop a pedestal, wrapped in a long police coat from his era with his hand outstretched, as if he is calling for order or trying to get someone's attention. Hay commemorates a bombing in which eight police officers were killed. The bomb was manufactured and tossed by a collection of socialist radicals. Competing narratives emerged from the bombing. The official narrative, the one most popular in the city, said the police in 1882 unleashed a vicious response in the wake of the attack, breaking into houses without warrants, manufacturing testimony and evidence. In the end, it was claimed that four men who were ultimately hanged for the bombing may have been innocent, framed by the corrupt police.

After almost a hundred years of the police abuse theory being the dominant narrative about the Haymarket bombing, writer Timothy Messer-Kruse turned it upside down. Messer-Kruse discovered new transcripts and records of the bombing investigation and trial. In these transcripts, Messer-Kruse concluded that the police and prosecutors had conducted a fair investigation. He also concluded that the police had treated the accused well, immediately letting some of them go when it was proven they were not involved, even if the accused had the most radical of résumés and were true revolutionaries. Those who were convicted were clearly guilty, Messer-Kruse said, and many other likely offenders got off because there was not enough evidence, including the bomb maker himself. Messer-Kruse's argument that the police were the ones who had been framed in the orthodox history of the bombing also applied to the exoneration of Anthony Porter, or the current manner by which attorneys for the NATO bombers were turning the tables on behalf of their terrorist clients.

I had purchased Messer-Kruse's book, impressed as I read it with how much the case explained my own misgivings about the wrongful conviction movement in my own time. Messer-Kruse discovered in his investigation of the bombing that the police seemed acutely aware that they were on a world stage, that they were being tested to see if they would function ethically. How would the police treat the men who were trying to destroy the city, and the country, through violence and misinformation? I tracked down Messer-Kruse at a midwestern university. He told me of the furious blowback he received from the academic community for challenging the mythology of police and prosecutorial corruption in the Haymarket bombing. His narrative was reassuring, revealing a pattern of false wrongful conviction claims from my own times to the early days of the city. The Weather Underground was nothing new. My conversation with Messer-Kruse also brought me back to the conversation with William Kennedy about Bill Ayers and the Weather Underground, to the wedge that divided me from fully embracing the magical realists, for whom socialist revolutionaries were still heroes.

For a long time after I talked with Messer-Kruse, I thought about sitting with Hay on a summer day and reading the book to him, or maybe in the winter during a storm so that Hay might know that his existence was not in vain, that somebody got it. I figured that after so many decades of standing around trying to let people know what truly happened, Hay would find it comforting that someone had actually dug up the evidence and found the true story. But, again, how would it look, a cop reading a book to a statue during a winter storm? The bosses would come out and benevolently lead me to the medical section and then to a psych evaluation. And so what if Hay understood that at least one academic had looked into the evidence of an alternate narrative? Nothing had really changed. Perhaps reading it to him would only depress him further, make him more angry. Perhaps he would snap and swat his powerful metal hand at some police hater walking into the building. They could easily die, being struck so. Then they would have to move Hay to some prison, where he would endure the sociopath's rant day and night, the way Jon Burge did when he was sentenced to four and a half years.

Cars were steadily arriving in the parking lot. Officers and civilian personnel walked by me, carrying their own equipment in case they too were sent out to the street. Everyone was tense, walking in an anxious solitude. I was trying to disguise my need to linger next to Hay, my mind turning over the unavoidable conclusion that murder cases from his era, murder cases holding the themes of explosion and fire, connected his era to mine. I set down my equipment next to Hay's pedestal and took a close look at him. His sense of duty impressed me. He stood outside headquarters all day and night. I wondered what it must be like in the winter winds, with his arm stretched out like that. I know from working as a doorman and then sitting on crime scenes as a cop how the biting cold can blow down the gap between one's clothing and skin. It goes up one's arm to the armpit, then down to the small of the back. Hay takes it. I couldn't. I would get on the radio and demand a break based on the union contract. Then I would go to the Starbucks on the corner and order a latte, sit in the corner, and warm up until a supervisor ordered me back.

I heard car doors slamming in the parking lot, more people arriving, but I still had some time, so I stayed with Hay. I knew how futile his whole life must seem for him, stuck hidden away in the parking lot of police headquarters. Yet he didn't give up, constantly reaching out to get someone's attention. No one really responds, only a few cops, and even then it is often only due to some holiday ceremony. The raising of his arm in a futile attempt to get people to listen may be prophetic for me as well, trying as I am to tell anyone who will listen that they have the whole city wrong, from the Haymarket bombing to this very day. Hay must feel he has wasted his time for more than a hundred years. His isolation in the parking lot reminds me of me trying to sell my book, my vain hope that it would catch the imagination of the Chicago citizens. If Hay can't do it, how can I? I once thought that my walking over to him was a sign of our solidarity, that it encouraged him, but I know now my presence must depress him even further: a single patrolman the only one listening?

Adding to Hay's woes is the fact that he is only a few feet from the side entrance to headquarters where convicted criminals, including sex offenders, must register. They mill about this entrance, all around the memorial, waiting for their turn to speak to an administrator inside. Whoever chose to put this office at police headquarters, near where the cops enter, had a dark sense of humor. It's no way to start one's day, a collection of pissed-off criminals glaring at you as you walk into work. It's much worse for Hay, though. He must endure these chronic offenders standing around him, leaning on him. Sometimes they smoke or put their butts out on him, and he never reacts. They leave their soda cans on the ledge of his pedestal. They curse, talk about their crimes without even noticing that he is listening. All day long he must listen to their sociopathic blather, their claims of innocence, that the cops framed them. Some of them are rapists.

Many are gang members. How many times a day does he hear the word "motherfucker"? I couldn't last a week up there. I'd be calling the FOP, saying this is bullshit. Get me the fuck out of here. How badly Hay must want to let his arm down and give these criminals a swift swat in the back of the head.

"Why don't you shut up, motherfucker, and admit you put yourself in this position?" he wants to say as they piss and moan about the injustice of the criminal case against them. "Pick up your cigarette butts, go stand in line, and shut the fuck up."

Hay never does that. He never climbs down from the pedestal and says, "Fuck this shit, I quit," and walks out of the parking lot to a nearby bar. Even in the worst storms at night, when the loneliness of his crusade must seem the most hopeless, he stays at his post. He doesn't sneak down from it late at night when there are few people around, the way so many cops sneak away from their post to get some chips and a Big Gulp at the 7-Eleven around the corner. Hay certainly knows he could go to the second floor where the vending machines are, buy some chips, and wait out the storm, reading the paper and warming his metal bones. No one would mess with him, not even the superintendent.

As I leaned against Hay, I recalled his history, tracing the fires and explosions of the revolutionaries from him to me. The Haymarket Memorial had originally stood at the site of the Haymarket bombing near the intersection of Des Plaines and Randolph. Then, at the 1968 riots during the Democratic National Convention, youths threw paint on him. In 1969 a group of youths, radicalized in their opposition to the

Vietnam War and the treatment of blacks, formed the
Weather Underground. They sent messengers all throughout
the country calling for the students to join them in Grant
Park to kick off this revolution, calling it the Days of Rage.
Expecting some 50,000 youths to show up, only about 200
actually appeared. On the first day, they placed a bomb
between the legs of the Haymarket Memorial and set it off,
destroying Hay. Recalling this bombing, I took a quick look
up at Hay, wondering if indeed he had been permanently
harmed, if you know what I mean, but then thought better of
it and looked downward again. The Weather Underground,
like the Black Panthers, would become closely tied to the
People's Law Office, the law firm later representing the
NATO bombers, claiming the arrest of their clients was a
police conspiracy.

It was perplexing to Hay and me that this connection
between the PLO and the Weather Underground wasn't
played up more by the media, the fact that the PLO's support
of so many revolutionary groups should illuminate evidence
of a bias against the police. More so, it was perplexing to us
why this connection didn't emerge in the newspaper stories
about the accused NATO bombers. Why wasn't the long
history of the PLO supporting terrorist groups mentioned in
media coverage of the PLO's defense of the accused NATO
bombers? Wasn't it clearly relevant, the way a history of
misconduct complaints against a detective was relevant?

After Hay was bombed between the legs, Mayor Daley,
the older one, had the statue rebuilt. The Weathermen
struck again. Exactly one year after the first bombing,
Weather Underground members blew Hay up again. Daley

had it rebuilt again. The following decade, the Weather Underground members would go on to set off bombs throughout the country, especially at police stations. Bernardine Dohrn graduated from the University of Chicago Law School, the same university that had published my first book but rejected the second book about the Porter case. The two ringleaders, Dohrn and William Ayers, would mastermind several of the bombings and carry them out. Eventually, they would marry. Both Ayers and Dohrn would become faculty members at Chicago universities. Dohrn would get a job at Northwestern, the school whose star journalism professor, David Protess, led the Innocence Project to free convicted killer Anthony Porter by a "confession" from what the evidence clearly showed was an innocent Alstory Simon. Later, she too would work on wrongful conviction cases.

The fate of the Haymarket Memorial and those of the Weather Underground terrorists made a telling contrast. Hay's fate seemed closer to my own. It eventually became clear even to Mayor Daley that the memorial could not reside in a public domain without being defaced or blown up, so it was relocated to the lobby of the old police headquarters at Eleventh and State. In this move, there was a kind of surrender. On the one hand, it is a statue calling for peace on the streets, for law and order in a most violent city, and, on the other, it could not safely be placed on those streets. The memorial was moved into secrecy, while its bombers moved into the public arena, to prestigious academic careers. And for more than a century, Hay had to endure a false narrative about what he stood for, about how he had come into being. When the old headquarters building was torn down, the memorial was moved yet again, this time to the police academy. It was here I first encountered Hay in a little grotto in a courtyard in the center of the building. Fellow classmates and I often ate lunch out there on warm sunny days. A few classmates once asked about it. Finally knowing something relevant in the academy, I chimed in with a brief history of the bombing, stating the official narrative, the only one I knew at the time, that innocent men may have been rounded up and killed in response to the bombing. Everyone just kind of looked at me when I said this. Many of my classmates were the offspring of police officers, and I had not yet learned how skeptical they were about official narratives claiming police misconduct.

Eventually, the memorial was placed at the back entrance of the new police headquarters at Thirty-Fifth and Michigan, where Hay and I were reunited, only now my mind was changing about who Hay was and what he stood for. Even this home at the new police headquarters was ignominious. Hay was not placed in front of the building where the public could see him on their way in and out. Instead, he lingered in the rear next to the secure parking lot used only by the police and their guests. Here at headquarters was where Hay and I were joined together, each of us an outcast from a common narrative.

I stood up straight, moved away from Hay, got ready to go into headquarters, not knowing what the day would hold. One purpose of myth is to provide a foothold on the past, to find an essential theme that will illuminate what is essential and meaningful. But Chicago's myths, I have learned, serve a more local purpose. They necessarily transform the past into agents of the city's corruption, compelling everyone to live within the landscape of some belligerent lie. How else could the city prevail from one generation to the next? As a result, one's imaginative life is never one's own, and largely false. The false narrative imposes a tragic force, for one learns, too late, one has been living a lie, a lie that has caused great harm. I looked up at the memorial. Both Hay and I live our lives outside city myths, trying to live according to a different narrative. Hay has suffered much more. He's been painted over, blown up twice, and is stuck in one position outside all day and night, in any weather. Meanwhile, I wonder if I am throwing my writing career away on a narrative so counter-revolutionary that no publisher, no person in the "legitimate" world, will publish it.

What it must have been like for Hay to have the Weather Underground members climb up on him and plant the explosives, their whispering, urgent voices. That must have been unbearable. Why didn't he beat them with the metal club hanging from his belt? Then they came back a year later. Perhaps, he figured, they would be brought to justice. Perhaps, he figured, they would spend their lives in prison and he would have the last laugh. Clearly, Hay had badly misconstrued his world, and certainly the city. How bitter he must have been when he learned that some of the radicals had escaped prison and obtained cushy jobs at Chicago universities while he sat in lobbies and then a parking lot, outside all day and night, without even lunch relief.

But now I wanted to talk to Hay, tell him about my

newfound enthusiasm. I wanted to tell him that I took an unconscionable reassurance in the emergence of the NATO bombers. The reason was that a metaphor was lingering in the ever-expanding collection of bomb plots and murder cases that called out to me, and a metaphor is the writer's dream. You see, I could not give expression to the connections I perceived among these crimes and plots across such a vast expanse of time until I applied the narrative of the detectives' investigation upon them. This is what brought to life the Porter case for me, what made it coherent and meaningful: when I sat down with the detectives in the case, listening spellbound as they described, step by step, their investigation of the case. But now that detective's method was becoming more specific, moving into that of a bomb and arson investigator, because the Porter case ultimately led me to an arson in which several people died, and the offender in this case, just like Porter, walked free from death row.

It is the arson investigator's primary duty to establish a "burn pattern" at the scene of a fire. This pattern establishes the pathway of an incendiary event from origin to conclusion. It provides the central legal theory of the crime, which will later be tested in court under the most intense cross-examination.

But for me, I was at that time beginning to perceive, without fully realizing it, a larger burn pattern at the core of the city, tying it together as only a metaphor can. Initially, this burn pattern became apparent to me, as it does to every cop, in the chronic intensity of the city, the pressure in which the city was always on the verge of an explosion in one form or another. But then it became more palpable, tying together seemingly disparate things like the Porter case in 1982, a group of would-be bombers planning to set the police on fire in the present time, and the Haymarket bombing in the city's ancient history. Most of all, the burn pattern traced the revolutionary fervor chronically simmering within the city. This pattern established the city's true imaginative boundaries, not its corrupt ones, from the real, to the imaginary and the fantastic, then back again. This notion stoked my own counterrevolutionary designs. Here was an imaginative freedom far more valuable than the success I tossed away as a writer by following this pattern, even if it meant embracing the worldview of detectives who had been deemed monsters in the city's corrupt imagination. That these would-be NATO bombers emerged at the same time this burn pattern was becoming palpable to me in the long history of the city was a sign that I was on the right track, with the right metaphor. This is why I found the bombers so reassuring.

It was in this simmering frame of mind that I gathered up my equipment. *Here it is 2012*, I thought. *The bombs are threatening again. I know I will never believe in city myths again, ever. Rather, I will trace these burn patterns, from Hay to me, and in between.* I looked up at him, nodded.

"Take it easy, brother."

Chapter 8

SUMMER HEAT

It was hot in my condo. All the windows were open, but
no breeze came in. Outside the sun was so bright, it was
difficult to see clearly. Every time my phone vibrated with a
new message or an incoming call, I snatched it up, hoping it
was news from the Cook County prosecutor, Anita Alvarez,
announcing she had completed an investigation into the
Anthony Porter murder case. Alvarez had initiated this
review grudgingly, after a group of us had presented her with
evidence that Porter was guilty, even though he had been
exonerated of the double murder in 1999. We also provided
evidence to Alvarez that the man who had confessed to the
crimes, Alstory Simon, was innocent. But it wasn't just the
release of Alstory Simon from prison that I sought. It was a
step into legitimacy for me, a sign that my vision of the city,
with what I perceived as its emerging burn patterns of the
revolution, was valid. And it would grant me legitimacy in a
grand manner, for the exoneration of Porter in 1999 had been

the crowning achievement in the wrongful conviction movement. So many killers were let out in the wake of his exoneration. All the while, Alstory Simon had wasted away in prison.

But, I wondered again in my condo, would Alvarez do it?
Would she let Simon out? In many ways, it would be so
much better for her to leave him in prison. One reason was
that declaring Simon's conviction a fraud would reveal
painful truths about the prosecutor's role in releasing Porter
and indicting Simon in 1999. The image that emerged from
the Porter case, then other cases, was that the prosecutor's
office was pressured by the media coverage of the cases, not
by the evidence produced in the courts. This media was
working closely with Protess, accepting his claims without
checking them. At the time Porter was released, the *Chicago
Tribune* had published a series of articles authored by
reporters, some of whom had attended Northwestern's journalism school, claiming scores of innocent people had been
convicted by prosecutors. It would be one of the first signs of
how wrongful conviction activists like Protess and the media
seemed to be working in concert. The articles sent the prosecutor's office into chaos, as they tried to defend their convictions. Then, right after these articles appeared, the *Tribune*
came forward with Protess's claims that Porter was innocent,
splashing the narrative of a man on death row, about to be
executed, who was actually innocent. The pressure proved
too much. An internal battle broke out in the prosecutor's
office, some top officials arguing that Porter should be
retried, despite the media hysteria. But in the end, the top
prosecutor at the time, Dick Devine, folded, and he ordered
Porter's release. Not only did Devine release Porter, but his

office declined to retry him. It was one of the first signs that prosecutors were responding more to the alliance of media and wrongful conviction activists than they were to the rule of evidence.

Releasing Simon would put a spotlight on this questionable decision by the prosecutor in 1999. But it would also ask basic questions about Alvarez's administration. If the conviction of Simon was faulty, why didn't her office see it earlier? Why didn't they take up his case years ago? And then there was the most difficult question of all: What was the prosecutor's role in other suspicious wrongful conviction claims? Those of us familiar with the case argued that the prosecutor's office bowed to media pressure in this and other cases and caved, a violation of their oath as prosecutors to try cases based on evidence.

But there was another purpose in getting Alstory Simon out of prison. At the very moment Alvarez was reviewing the Porter/Simon case, former Chicago Police commander Jon Burge was in prison for allegedly lying about torturing confessions from suspects over the course of several decades. Burge had become the icon of police torture and corruption. There was a palpable fear among many in the city, including the prosecutors, that the unraveling of the Porter case would lead back to the Burge conviction and cast doubt on it. If wrongful conviction activists had lied about the Porter case and framed an innocent man in Alstory Simon, there was a question lingering throughout the entire city: How many cases had they lied about? How many killers had been set free? Did the evidence of corruption in the Porter case go all the way back to the Burge case?

This was the nether world I lived in, the one between knowing Porter was guilty, Simon innocent, and getting one facet of the city's institutions to admit it. I looked at myself sitting in my messy condo, court transcripts everywhere, police reports. I reached down and scratched myself. Alvarez's review of the Alstory Simon case was now in its ninth month, with no end in sight. In this heat, simmering in my own anxiety and self-doubt, I moved back into the perspective of the detectives again, as a kind of safe haven, for their investigations were the only means by which I might comprehend what was taking place. The Porter story from the detective's perspective established a line, with solid evidence and testimony, connecting an offender to the victim. The realism of this line was initially tested in the city's courts, under the rules of evidence. But then sixteen years later, the line of this evidence was corrupted when Professor Protess, private investigator Ciolino, and Protess's students announced that the real shooter was another man, Alstory Simon. They packaged this false narrative with the help of media allies, packed together its bellicose, unreal elements, then hurled it at a city whose institutions were already so corrupted they could not withstand the attack.

These cases were revolutionary, far more successful than the bomb throwing of earlier decades. For after the Porter case, the city moved into a new imaginative world, one in which any murder case, any one at all, could itself be transformed. The entire order of the city changed. Everything. But the detectives remained bound to the essential, mundane lines connecting Porter to the murder of Hillard and Green. For them, this line could not be obfuscated, could not be ignored. As a writer, I wanted to be bound to these mundane lines as well. The reason is that there was a grave, unspoken injustice in these exonerations, a brutal, violent, and burning cruelty, one that undermined the contemporary guise of social justice and higher principle justifying these exonerations and tied its advocates to the bombings of yesteryear. But now these exonerations were orthodox history, the mythology of the established order and we were enveloped in it. Realizing this, I felt as if I were roasting in the summer heat of my condo, ruminating on the history of the city and the ascendance of the wrongful conviction movement. My mind raced. It was too late. I was insignificant. Would a firebomb come flying through my window? Would a gunshot explode through it into my chest? Would Alvarez leave Alstory Simon in prison?

With the now-viable chance of Alstory Simon being set free from prison, the cops' take on city murders initiated its own revolutionary vision, revealing that the magical and the real were not, as the bomb throwers' mythology maintained, working in sympathy, not really. In fact, they were vying with one another, vying desperately and violently, and always had been. It was absolutely crucial for me as a cop and a writer to get the narrative right, to follow the murders the way the detectives did, none more so than in the Porter case. The Porter murders were a starting place, asking what was now the central question in the city: Who shot Marilyn Green and Jerry Hillard? An official declaration by Alvarez that Simon was innocent—or even his release from prison—could initiate a revolution of another kind, for freeing Simon would also bring forth that essential question: If the Anthony

Porter case was dirty, if it was little more than a bomb hurled at the criminal justice system, how many others were? Here was an emerging pattern that offered up what was truly magical and counterrevolutionary: a wholly uncorrupted vision of the city.

I liked that notion. I liked it a great deal.

The sun moved over the roof of my courtyard building, spilling a white light in my windows, then onto my computer. I could barely see the screen. It would last only a few minutes, so I got up and retreated from it, then returned. I was gambling a lot in investigating these murder cases, in trying to get Alstory Simon out of prison. I could see the city coming after me, my police job in jeopardy, and I had black-listed myself as a writer by calling out the local media in their failure to address the facts of the Porter case. My grand hopes sank. I was going nowhere, only simmering in the city fires. I was counting on a state's attorney, a prosecutor, doing the right thing in the face of so much political pressure to do the wrong thing.

It was worse than that. Perhaps for all my high hopes and dreams, I didn't even know what was truly happening to me, just as the students who worked with Protess could not know what they were truly getting involved in. Perhaps I was becoming nothing more than a bomb thrower myself, my writing hurled at my enemies in the same manner and with the same intent with which they hurled their claims about the murder cases at the police and the courts. Bomb throwing; it seemed an inescapable condition. Was it true? Were my intentions any more noble than my enemies'? Here I was sitting in my apartment unshowered, unshaven, filled with dark foreboding and anger, vengeful. Who was I? It was still bright in my apartment, but I could see the computer screen again. I leaned forward on my desk, taking care not to drip any sweat onto the keypad. I knew all about desolation and dark intent, for I became aware that I was living the revolutionary's life as well, always plotting. I kept telling myself, as all good revolutionaries did, that my counterrevolution was different, that I was working toward a greater good. I knew full well that the crusade to release Simon from prison and to take on the forces of Northwestern, the media, the entire city—if successful—held its own force of the magical, and I was enthralled by the possibility of it. But I also knew that, in the heart of a true revolutionary, ideas often became second to the allure of the destruction itself, to the thrill of the bombing. Often they became merely the excuse for it. Was that me? Was that what I was becoming? It was easy to tell myself that I was using these murders for my own creative enterprise, but in truth was I only embarked on a mission of destruction, just as they were?

I wiped my face with a paper towel that was lying on my desk. My T-shirt was wet. There was still no breeze. Soon I would take a cold shower and get ready for work. In my most intense self-doubt, I wondered if I was simply throwing my life away, in particular my writing life, if this were all a dead end. Well, the question was largely pointless. I was in too deep now. I had to toss aside the dark fears and sentiments I held about my own revolution. It would only get worse. I knew that. I had to move deeper into the burn patterns, for

well I knew there was an evolution in them, and I sensed that
the Porter case was merely an introduction into a larger
world. So as I waited for a phone message about Alvarez's
decision on Simon, I walked over to a large table that took up
much of my living room, stacked with boxes of transcripts
and documents in various other boxes. I took the lid off the
box marked "Wilson Brothers" and began pulling out the
case and detectives' reports on another double homicide,
one that took place about six months before Porter's double
murder, the same year, 1982.

Andrew and Jackie Wilson were driving southbound on
Morgan at Eighty-First Street on a bitterly cold winter
morning in 1982 when they were observed by two officers,
William Fahey and Richard O'Brien. Fahey and O'Brien were
not regular partners, and they were not dressed in their
regular uniforms. Instead, they were wearing their formal
uniforms because they had attended a funeral that morning,
a funeral for a rookie policeman who had been gunned
down four days earlier on a bus by a man named Edgar
Hope. The entire department was devastated by the murder
of this rookie police officer. He had a family, was just starting
out in his career. What added to their grief was also a sense
of terror. The reason was that a few weeks before Edgar
Hope had shot this rookie officer, two other officers had been
gunned down. In that shooting, a man had barged into a
McDonald's and caused a commotion. Two off-duty Cook
County sheriffs were working security at the restaurant. They
approached the man. When they did, another offender

entered the restaurant with a shotgun and gunned down one of the sheriffs. The offender who had walked in first knocked the other sheriff to the ground and raised a gun to the sheriff's head. Witnesses said the offender was smiling. Right before the offender pulled the trigger, the sheriff raised his hand. The offender fired, but the bullet ricocheted off the sheriff's hand and went into his mouth, wounding but not killing him. The sheriff pretended he was dead. The two offenders then fled the scene. This meant that in just a few weeks, three police officers had been shot, two of them fatally. Now, only four days after the rookie police officer was shot and weeks after the two off-duty sheriffs had been shot, Andrew and Jackie Wilson were driving on the South Side, across the path of Fahey and O'Brien.

Jackie and Andrew Wilson were career thugs, gang members guilty of everything from robbery to burglary to felony batteries. Once they had posed as mailmen, broke into the home of an old woman, tied her up, robbed and beat her. When they crossed Eighty-First Street in front of Fahey and O'Brien, they were getting ready for another crime, this the most daring of all. They were headed to Cook County Hospital, where they were going to spring their friend Edgar Hope from police custody. Hope was in the hospital because he had been wounded when he had shot the rookie cop on the bus four days earlier, the cop whose funeral Fahey and O'Brien had attended earlier that day. Andrew and Jackie realized that only a few cops would be guarding Hope at the hospital. It would be relatively easy to break him out. In the back of the Wilsons' car were nurse uniforms they would use to enter the hospital in disguise. Earlier that day, they had broken into a home, one they thought was owned by a police officer, in the hopes that they could find more guns and ammunition, but they came up empty. Now the brothers crossed Eighty-First Street, spied by two cops who had just come from the funeral of a cop murdered by the man the Wilsons were about to spring from custody. What happened next would make the sense of terror that cops were experiencing legitimate, official even.

A man standing at the window of his home watched the whole thing unfold. Fahey and O'Brien pulled over the Wilsons' car and approached it, O'Brien on the driver's side, Fahey on the passenger's. As O'Brien approached, Jackie Wilson exited the car from the driver's side, never a good sign. Fahey pulled Andrew Wilson out of the passenger side. While O'Brien was talking to Jackie, Andrew tried to reach into the car, ostensibly to get his jacket. Fahey stopped him, grabbed the jacket, and began fingering through it. He found some ammunition. O'Brien then found the pistol in the front seat and announced it to his partner. Andrew, who already had a warrant out for his arrest and was looking at a long prison term, swung around on Fahey and began wrestling for Fahey's pistol. They moved toward the back of the car and slipped on the ice. Andrew came up with Fahey's weapon. He shot Fahey in the back of the head. Unable to shoot because his partner was wrestling with Andrew, O'Brien, holding two guns, the one he found in the car and his own, also had to watch Jackie Wilson. After Andrew shot Fahey, Andrew crouched behind the rear of the car, fired across it, and hit O'Brien in the chest. Andrew, keeping Fahey's pistol, told his brother to grab O'Brien's gun as well.

"But he is still alive," Jackie told his brother.

So Andrew jumped up on the rear of the vehicle, looming over O'Brien on the ground. The last image of O'Brien's life was that of a psychotic criminal raising his partner's pistol and firing three more times into his chest. O'Brien and Fahey had just foiled, without knowing it, a plot to free from custody another killer, a plot, if implemented, that could have cost the lives of many more people. The Wilson brothers got into their car. As they did so, a witness pulling up said Andrew was laughing. Another witness arrived on the scene and grabbed the microphone in the squad car. He called out that two cops had been shot. This message went across much of the South Side to cops who had just returned from a police funeral. None of the police knew at this point about the connection between the Wilsons and Hope, the fact that Andrew and Jackie were going to spring the guy who had killed the rookie cop from Cook County Hospital, where Hope was recovering from gunshots in the shootout on the bus. But the police knew something had changed in the city, something had fundamentally moved away from them and on to the side of the killers: they had all just returned from the funeral of a murdered rookie cop, and now here was the unfamiliar voice of a civilian yelling into the microphone that two more cops had been shot. Police arrived. The wagon carried Fahey and O'Brien to the hospital, where both would succumb to their wounds.

Now, in a fantastic manner, the evidence began to emerge connecting the murders. The detectives slowly learned about the Wilsons' plan to spring Hope from prison. But there was something just as incredible that came to light. Investigators would also run two guns found on Hope when he was taken into custody outside the bus where he had killed the rookie policeman. One of those guns was identified as the gun that was used to shoot a sheriff a few weeks earlier at a McDonald's, the first clue that Hope was responsible for that murder as well. Detectives eventually figured out that Andrew Wilson and Edgar Hope were responsible for murdering four cops and shooting five in less than a month.

Jon Burge was assigned the murders of Fahey and O'Brien. An aggressive cop with strong contacts on the street, Burge also held the respect of the men he commanded as well as the respect of the command staff. They relied on him for tough cases like the Fahey and O'Brien murders. Cops all over the city came in on their days off to pitch in. They found Wilson's car. Then they got a tip days later that Andrew Wilson was hiding out in an apartment on the West Side. Early in the morning four days after the murders, Burge and his men went there and took Andrew Wilson into custody. Wilson was taken back to Area 2. His brother Jackie was also found that day in another part of the city. Eventually both men confessed. They were transported to another location for a lineup where a witness identified Andrew Wilson, then brought back again to Area 2. A state's attorney came and took another confession.

Later than night, Burge called for a wagon to transport Andrew Wilson to central lockup downtown. The wagon men arrived. As they escorted Wilson out, he said to one of them, "I should have killed more of you pigs." When the wagon men brought Wilson to the lockup downtown, he was badly beaten. Wilson was bruised on his face and body. The bruises were bad enough that the lockup keeper would not accept him without a medical release, so the two wagon men took him to Mercy Hospital, where, by all accounts, one of the cops became unhinged. He began threatening Wilson and pulled his gun on him, pointing it at him and cursing him out. The doctor was alarmed and told the officer he wouldn't treat Wilson if the officer had his gun out. The doctor observed all the bruises on Wilson, saying some of them were burns, and documented them. The officers brought Wilson back to the lockup all bandaged up. The following day, the doctor at the county jail also documented Wilson's injuries and wrote a letter to the police superintendent stating he believed that Wilson had been abused.

The law firm that took up Andrew Wilson's case was the People's Law Office, the same law firm that would defend some of the NATO bombers during my own career. PLO lawyers blamed Burge, not the wagon men, for Wilson's abuse. This was an argument that struck cops as ludicrous for a host of reasons. Burge and his men found Wilson four days after the killings. Fahey and O'Brien had already been buried. Burge was in contact with the families every day, keeping them apprised of their investigation. How foolish it would be, what a betrayal of the families, if Burge and his men tortured Wilson, leaving so many marks on him and providing an instant defense to a cop killer. It would also be a betrayal of the entire police department, as many of them wanted Wilson to face the death penalty. But equally important was the fact that giving Wilson a defense would infuriate police officers. Burge and his men already had an open-and-shut case against Wilson. They didn't need a confession.

While it may be possible to imagine Burge and his men would have attacked Wilson if they had discovered him the day of the shooting, unable to contain their rage, the claim that they would do so four days later as their investigation was under way was difficult to imagine, let alone prove in court.

A far more compelling explanation for Wilson's abuse is the likelihood that it was done by the wagon men who picked him up and who had an opportunity to be alone with Wilson. But this narrative would not serve the motives of the PLO. At the time of the Fahey and O'Brien murders, the PLO was searching for relevance. The law firm had been founded to represent the Black Panthers, then later they represented the Puerto Rican liberation organization, the FALN, which committed more than one hundred bombings throughout the country that killed civilians and police officers. The FALN was considered by the FBI to be the most violent domestic terrorist group. The PLO's relationship to the members of these organizations was more than just as lawyer. In their writings about this era and these groups, there was a deep ideological sympathy and solidarity with these clients. This intensely radical political agenda, tied to violent terrorist groups, never garnered the PLO much popular support. By the end of the 1970s, the Black Panthers no longer existed. The country was fed up with Weather Underground bombings and their calls for revolution. But Andrew Wilson's wounds, if they were from cops torturing him for a confession, provided the law firm with a new opportunity to attack the police. Nevertheless, in the local media, the PLO's long association with terrorist organizations that had killed people, including cops, was rarely discussed in the context of their accusations against the police. The signs of an intense anti-police bias at the heart of the PLO was rarely mentioned in the media, though cops railed against it. The PLO pinned Wilson's abuse on Burge and his men: the notion of a white racist cop in a black neighborhood, running around torturing confessions out of suspects, fulfilled the image of the Chicago Police that activists like the PLO had been pushing since the 1968 riots in Chicago, and even back to the Haymarket riots, when the police were accused of framing the socialists involved.

At first, few people would listen to PLO claims about Burge and the Wilson case. The main lawyer at the firm, G. Flint Taylor, pressed his claims about Burge over and over. Twice he sued Burge for torturing Wilson. During both trials, Taylor's antics in the courtroom revealed an "anything to win" strategy by him and his supporters. Taylor was hit with several contempt charges. Once again, the media refused to bring up the PLO's support of violent terrorists, their staunch anti-American rhetoric, and their sympathy with self-avowed Marxist activists. In the first trial, Burge's men were exonerated, but the jury was hung on a verdict against Burge himself. In the retrial, the jury admitted that Wilson had been abused, and that there was a policy of abuse against suspects in police murders, but the jury acquitted Burge himself, an admission that they couldn't be sure who abused Wilson. One street-smart juror even suggested that Wilson may have abused himself in an effort to build a defense. But despite these two defeats in the courts, Taylor displayed an energy and focus common to the most die-hard zealots. He

pressed on with his campaign against Burge, this time
outside the courts. He corralled his colleagues and
supporters into a massive media blitz. There were demonstrations outside the home of Mayor Daley, chanting, "Hey
hey, ho ho, Jon Burge has got to go."

Taylor also enjoyed one other crucial advantage. Ever
since his PLO had organized itself around the Black
Panthers, it had forged deep connections within the city's
powerful black caucus, a collection of aldermen, religious
leaders, and activists that controlled the black political structure, including the black vote, in the city. This caucus began
to make rumbles about Burge and Daley's unwillingness to
go after him, a sign that Daley might lose this core
constituency. One card the black caucus had played against
Daley was the fact that the mayor had been the lead prosecutor in the city in 1982, when Wilson gunned down Fahey
and O'Brien. Daley's failure to take action about certain
evidence of police abuse in the case was a weak spot, a
powerful piece of leverage against a mayor who desperately
needed the black vote to stay in power.

Daley took the bait. He made Burge the fall guy. The
mayor employed a common tactic in machine politics. He
imposed a new leader in the agency that oversees misconduct of the police department. Daley's handpicked new
leader of the agency, called the Office of Professional Stan-
dards (OPS), initiated yet another investigation into the
Wilson case and others, and suddenly declared there was
evidence in these cases of abuse by Burge and his men. Nine
years earlier, the same agency had refused disciplinary
measures against Burge. The police, the police union, and

the attorneys working for them were furious at this move by Daley. Nevertheless, with this declaration by OPS that Burge was the monster that the PLO and all their radical allies had been saying he was, the case against Burge and his men moved to a police board, a collection of civilians also appointed by the mayor. In a series of hearings in front of this board, Wilson testified that he was beaten and burned by Burge and his men. The police board hearings were the fourth time the family of Fahey and O'Brien had to sit through testimony by Wilson.

At the end of it, the police board fired Burge. Taylor and his movement against the police had taken its first step into legitimacy. Andrew Wilson was a hero in the prison system, a kind of godfather to every inmate looking for a way out. Burge left Chicago and moved to Florida, regularly called up to Chicago for depositions as one inmate after another began making the same claims against him as Wilson did. These inmates began filing lawsuits. The city began settling them; Taylor's law firm, the PLO, and then other allied law firms raked in millions. The revolution was not only saved—it was funded.

What was an added burden to me in learning about the Wilson case was the timing of it, February 1982. It was the same month and year in which I ignominiously returned to Chicago, hitchhiking into the city from Kalamazoo, Michigan, where I was flunking out of college. It was in Kalamazoo that I first took some literature classes and the vague notion of becoming a writer first entered my mind, and when I moved to Chicago a decade later, the desire to write about Chicago moved to the forefront. But the kid who hitchhiked to Chicago in February 1982 was a long way from being able to see the Andrew Wilson murders with any clarity, was a long way from being able to see that perhaps Burge and his men were innocent of the charges against them, that the city's universities and law firms could be far more culpable of corruption than the police.

The PLO's claims about Burge torturing Wilson precipitated what eventually became known as the wrongful conviction movement, driven by the claim that the police were evil racists in Chicago and had been torturing and abusing suspects for decades. The question of what really happened in these cases therefore became crucial for me. As this movement took shape and expanded throughout the city, then beyond, my growing doubt about the PLO's claims suggested to me that I had lived much of my life under a great lie, for, at the time that Wilson had killed Fahey and O'Brien, I would have wholeheartedly believed the torture narrative posed by Taylor and the PLO had I heard it, and I believed the subsequent claims about Burge all the years I had lived in the city, up until I became a cop. I began to think of my movement into the police department as fateful, not for me as a cop, but as a writer, as if the police job offered the one chance of obtaining something I had always sought in the city, something all writers covet: a way into something indisputably authentic. For if the claims about Burge and his men were false, then the entire city was living in a dreadful, violent lie. In these crimes, I concluded, I might overcome the central corruption of the city itself, the fact that it holds our imaginations hostage in some lie, even when we don't realize it, as if our imaginations are not our own. I began to wonder, like a

revolutionary, whether I could change this and take possession of my own imagination. To do so, I must inevitably go
deeper into the burn patterns, to an arson committed in 1987.
For there, at that mass murder, I had discovered that all burn
patterns in the city merged.

So while waiting for a phone call about the decision of
Alvarez on the Porter case, I set down the files on the Wilson
murders and picked up the files I had accumulated of that
mass murder. I ferreted out the detectives' reports and interviews; in the cause of my own revolution, I had come to
believe that these were the most authentic records I could
find, perhaps the only authentic records in the city.

Chapter 9

HOBLEY ARSON

A rea 2 Homicide detectives Bob Dwyer and James Lotito were called to the scene of a fire on the South Side of Chicago on January 6, 1987. At the time of the arson, Anthony Porter was awaiting his execution on death row. Andrew Wilson and Jackie Wilson were also in prison. The claims that Burge and his men had brutalized Andrew Wilson were taking shape.

Bomb and arson investigators were already at the crime scene. Homicide detectives were called in because there were multiple deaths and because it had been determined that the fire was intentionally set, making all the deaths murders. It was one of the worst crime scenes any investigator had ever seen. The fire had raged swiftly through a three-story building with approximately twenty-two units in a working-class African American section of the city. When Lotito and Dwyer arrived, only three bodies had been found so far. Two of the three were a mother and her one-year-old child, Anita and Philip Hobley, found next to each other in apartment 301, a corner apartment just at the top of the stairs. Fire investigators told Lotito and Dwyer that an accelerant had been poured outside the Hobley apartment door and down the stairwell. Firefighters would eventually reveal that they smelled gasoline when they arrived. Investigators believed the fire had then been ignited from somewhere near the bottom of the stairs and raced up toward the Hobley apartment. The offender had not simply poured a pool of gas outside the Hobley apartment door on the third floor, investigators determined. He had soaked the apartment door and poured some underneath it so that it seeped into the apartment. From the earliest moments of the investigation, it looked as if the Hobley apartment had been targeted.

Anita and Philip Hobley never really had a chance. Within moments after the fire was lit, it raced up the stairs to the pool of gasoline outside their apartment, engulfing the door and seeping underneath it. Thick dark smoke immediately billowed into their apartment. Investigators said that the stairwell created a chimney effect, so that it spread quickly, as did the intense heat it generated. Detectives learned that a man lived in the apartment with Anita and Philip. He was the husband and father, Madison Hobley, but his body had not yet been found. Detectives figured Madison Hobley's body would eventually be discovered, but it wasn't. Detectives would eventually learn that seven people perished, two of them children. Seventeen others were injured. One man was badly burned and spent months in the hospital undergoing numerous skin grafts and operations. Other victims had broken backs or broken bones because they were forced to jump from the second and third floors. Several children were tossed from the upper floors to people below, who caught them. At the apartment building, the radios were crackling and the engines running. Groups of people were standing huddled outside, wrapped in blankets or extra clothes because of the cold.

Crimes scenes with so many killed and injured require dozens of investigators from different units, often investigators who don't know one another. The victims were scattered across the South Side, at the scene, hospitals, and the morgue. Detectives have multiple duties, including sorting out witnesses and victims. They would have to determine who lived where. Amidst the loud roar of the diesel engines from the Fire Department and the radios of firemen and police officers, they would listen to the fire investigators tell them what they knew about the arson. They also had to notify family members about the deaths of their loved ones. Some of the family members got word of the fire and appeared at the morgue or the hospital, and the detectives would have to break the news to them there. Anyone could be a suspect, anyone a key witness. Detectives had to make notifications to the 911 center, keep track of where each victim went, and give all this information to whoever was doing the initial case report. They had to keep the 911 center informed of where they were going. The case was also passed on to other detectives from different shifts, called watches. The magnitude of the crime quickly drew the media, who followed the police around in vans with cameras, hoping to get the first glimpse of a suspect on film.

Everyone at the fire scene—the firemen, the detectives

and patrolmen, those who had escaped, the family members arriving—they all would linger around the crime scene with a sense of the deep tragedy, having to face the horror of what the dead had gone through, trapped as the smoke and heat rushed in and there was no way out. Many of them witnessed the firefighters carrying the bodies out, including those of the two children. Two of the firefighters had been injured, though it wasn't life threatening. Firefighters testified at the trial about getting low in the hallway and feeling their way down, discovering bodies. What would it be like to grope down a smoke-filled hallway and touch the body of a dead child, pull it toward yourself, and carry the little corpse outside? They rescued many people, just barely pulling them from upper-floor windows before the fire would engulf them.

But all the evidence gathered from the fire, from firefighters and investigators, and from witness interviews would count for nothing. For what would ultimately take precedence in this arson was not a trial based on the rules of evidence but instead on the influence of a mythology already taking shape in the Wilson and Porter cases. By 1987, the time of the fire, this mythology was only a murmur throughout the city, but it was gaining traction. It was the notion that the police were racist monsters and the cops would take any case, even a mass murder like this one, and fuck it up to satisfy their racist rage. It was based on the bruises Andrew Wilson bore when he arrived with the wagon men at central lockup. A group of fringe activists—the same ones who would later defend the would-be bombers at the NATO demonstrations during my own career—would repeat over and over that an entire police unit headed by Jon Burge took part in Wilson's abuse. To them, it was not just a few distraught wagon men who abused Wilson for murdering Fahey and O'Brien, patrolmen who could not handle the fact that five Chicago police officers had been gunned down in less than a month. This mythology rejected the narrative that these men beat Wilson because they could not control their sorrow and anger in the hidden basement of headquarters or the back of the wagon. Instead, to these activists, it was a police conspiracy from the very top, one that every cop and supervisor was in on, and, no one, not one cop, would break the code of silence.

Lotito and Dwyer, of course, could not know this. At the scene of the fire, they interviewed fire investigators. These investigators told them that when they arrived, the hallway and stairwell were fully engulfed. They also told the detectives that two doors, an outer and an inner one, at the entrance of the building were locked. Because of this, firefighters had to make a forced entry. This was a compelling fact. If someone who did not live at the building set the fire, how did they get inside? It's possible they had a key or someone let them in, but it was also a sign that the fire could have been set by someone who lived in the building. The fire investigators also told the detectives that they believed the gasoline had been poured on the Hobleys' apartment door and in front of it, then down the stairs to the first floor.

Each group of detectives took up some aspect of the investigation. Dwyer and Lotito, who had worked with Burge during their career and would therefore later be dubbed "Burge detectives," went to the morgue to take notes and collect evidence on the bodies. They took the badly shaken

building manager along with them to help identify the
bodies. At the morgue, they met Myra Hobley, who had
arrived to identify her sister-in-law, Anita Hobley. Myra told
detectives that her brother, Madison, had escaped the fire
and was at their mother's house on the 8000 block of South
Rhodes Street. Myra provided the first account of Madison
Hobley's actions during the fire. She told detectives that
Hobley said he awoke to smoke and an alarm going off.
Hobley then went to the front door of the apartment and
then into the hallway, but could not get back inside because
the heat and smoke were too intense. Myra said her brother
went down the back stairs in the hopes of getting his wife
and son to jump out the window.

Myra told the detectives other information about
Hobley's actions after the fire. After he had arrived at his
mother's house, which was just a few blocks from his apartment, Myra said that the family had called the fire department because they wanted to get Hobley a tranquilizer. She
said Madison needed one because he was so upset about the
loss of his son and wife. Myra told the detectives that the
paramedics arrived and took Hobley to the hospital, but the
doctor at the emergency room refused to give him any sedative, saying there was no medical basis. Furious, Myra went
off on the doctor and left the hospital with Hobley, returning
to their mother's home on South Rhodes.

The detectives, somewhat surprised that Madison had
survived, dropped off the building manager near the crime
scene and headed to Hobley's mother's apartment. Hobley
was now the best lead in the case, as he had escaped from
where the fire had originated. Perhaps he might provide

telling clues. Perhaps he saw or heard something. Perhaps he could provide some information about anyone who was angry with him or his family, some dispute he was involved in, like gambling debts or problems with a local gang. The first person the detectives met at the apartment was Madison's mother, who directed them to her son in the rear. Lotito and Dwyer identified themselves to Madison and gave their condolences. Throughout the house there were Hobley family members along with family members of his wife, Anita, all wailing over the death of Madison's wife and son. Their loud crying and lamenting made it difficult for the detectives to converse with Hobley. They asked Hobley to move to the front of the apartment, away from the noise of the relatives. It was still too noisy in the front of the apartment for the detectives to talk with Hobley, so they suggested they all three go outside. Hobley agreed. As they walked out the door of the apartment, Hobley stopped, then went back inside. Hobley retrieved a bag with some clothes in it and handed it to the detectives, telling them that his mother told him to take a bath and to preserve the clothes because detectives would probably want them. Puzzled, the detectives took the bag. It was a strange gesture, to hand clothes to the detectives without any prompting.

Now outside on the porch, it was cold. Hobley began shivering, so the detectives suggested sitting in the warm police car. Dwyer took the bag of clothes Hobley had handed him and put them in the trunk. Inside the car, Detective Dwyer informed Hobley that the investigators believed the fire had been intentionally set. Dwyer asked Hobley if he knew of any conflicts in the building that may have been the source of the arson. At first Hobley answered by describing how he had escaped the fire. Hobley said he worked for a company that delivered medical equipment. He told the detectives he had undergone some paramedic training and this helped him survive. This training taught him to stay low on the ground. Then Hobley described in detail how he got out, but not his wife and child. He said he awoke smelling smoke. He woke up his wife, then went to the front door and walked out of it. Hobley said the smoke was coming from the rear of the building on the second floor and he walked toward it to investigate. He said he walked down the hallway, then tried to return to the apartment, but it was too hot, so he crawled down the back stairs and out, hoping to get his wife and child to jump from their apartment.

Then Hobley dropped a bomb. He told the detectives that there had been another fire set in the hallway outside his door about a week earlier, on New Year's Eve. This fire, Hobley said, was suspicious. Hobley said he was working at the time of this New Year's Eve fire. Next came another bombshell. The detectives asked Hobley if he knew anyone who might have set the fire. To their amazement, Hobley said yes. He fingered his mistress as the possible offender in both arsons. He explained to the detectives that his mistress, Angela McDaniel, was furious over their breakup, for Hobley's decision to break off his affair with her and remain with his wife, who was now dead. Hobley gave a reason why he suspected Angela for the first fire. He said that he mentioned this first fire, the one on New Year's Eve, to her during a meeting. According to Hobley, McDaniel said, "Oh, you mean the fire on the third floor." How did she know where the fire was, Hobley asked the detectives rhetorically, for he had never mentioned the location to her. This was the main reason why he now suspected her for the second arson as well, he told the detectives.

In the back of the car, Hobley went on to describe in more detail the nature of the affair he was having with McDaniel. He told the detectives how angry she was when Hobley told her she had to move out of the apartment so he could move back in with his wife and child. As Hobley spoke about McDaniel, the detectives realized they might have made a major breakthrough in the case. In response to Hobley's statements, the detectives asked him to come back to Area 2 to answer more questions, particularly about McDaniel. They needed information on how they could contact her. There was another reason detectives wanted to leave the location. The case attracted so much attention that the media was following detectives around in large vans. Dwyer and Lotito could not talk to Hobley without the prying eyes of the journalists, who were trying to obtain footage for their stories by filming detectives interviewing witnesses. Vans were constantly pulling up to the detectives' car. Hobley agreed to go with the detectives back to Area 2, the same location where Andrew and Jackie Wilson were taken after they were captured for killing Officers Fahey and O'Brien five years earlier.

It is this ride to the station that was, in my mind, pivotal for Hobley. He was going back to Area 2 with seasoned detectives who had worked hundreds of homicides. An arson had just killed seven people, including children, and now he was going to put the course of his life on the line with his flimsy story. His family members who had been supporting him were gone now. He was all alone. Clearly, he could imagine, there was forensic evidence of the crime surfacing. How would his story hold up against it? Hobley was also no doubt exhausted. There was the fire, the rescue scene afterward, going to his mother's house, then the hospital, back to his mother's, waiting for the police. He had not slept the entire night. Now he was in the back of the car, talking to the detectives. Soon he would arrive at the well-lit police district, walk into the bustling station. He would be placed in a room, the detectives coming and going, asking him polite questions. And it would all be on the line then, man, all on the line. I had seen it many times, seen the fortitude of many criminals, even gang members, wane as soon as they were out of the comfort zone of their friends and their turf, merely by entering the station and considering what they had done and the penalties involved. Seven people murdered, including children, one being Hobley's own son. That would be an awful lot to bear, even for the most hardened killer, which Hobley clearly was not. Hobley was a working person, with no rap sheet, and he was probably aware that in 1987 there was still the death penalty.

Hobley's drive to Area 2 with Lotito and Dwyer reminded me of an early experience on the job. I was working downtown, just out of the academy, on a beautiful summer day when my partner and I got a call to assist two detectives at a large skyscraper. I had never had a call like this before, meeting detectives somewhere. We went to a building near where the Chicago River met Lake Michigan, a building made up of fancy condos far beyond my financial means. Each condo had an extended porch high over the city, the lake, and the river. The detectives told us they had a warrant for a woman who lived inside. She had apparently stolen more than a quarter of a million dollars over the course of a few years from an ex-employer where she had worked as an accountant. She had, they said, skimmed the money with complicated accounting scams. The employer had only discovered it by accident, and even then it took a long time to figure out exactly how she had done it. The woman, the detectives said, probably figured she had gotten away with it because so much time had passed. They showed us the warrant, then said they needed us to transport her to a West Side station. We nodded, walked into the building with them, and took the elevator to a higher floor. The four of us stood outside the apartment door in the late morning. We could hear some movement inside and some soft music on the radio, like Frank Sinatra or something. I could smell coffee. It seemed as if she was enjoying herself, a beautiful morning, music, coffee. We paused a moment longer. Then the detective reached up to the door and knocked three times. There was a silence I will never forget. It was the first sound of her life suddenly falling apart. Then an almost-quavering voice, "Who is it?"

It's the knock on the door you have dreaded all these years, I thought.

The door opened slowly by a middle-aged woman

wearing a robe. The smell of the coffee was much stronger. There were large bay windows in the living room overlooking the lake, art along the walls.

"How can I help you?" she said, still hoping it was something about a parking ticket or even a stolen car, or some problem with a neighbor. That would be fine, just great.

"Ma'am, we're the Chicago Police. I'm a detective. We have a warrant for your arrest," said one of the detectives, flashing his badge.

"A warrant?" she said, feigning innocence that was betrayed in every line of her face. "What for?"

"I can't go into that right now, but I'm sure if you give it some thought, you can imagine why we're here," the detective said. "You need to gather some clothes."

She didn't argue or protest further, a clear sign of her guilt. If she were innocent, she would be going nuts. We stepped into the apartment, then my partner and I followed the woman when she went to another room, in case she got some crazy notion of grabbing a gun and shooting us or herself. Her closet was filled with nice clothes. I wondered if she had engaged in these crooked accounting schemes at other jobs. As we walked from room to room, she asked the usual panicked questions about what to bring, the detective telling her only clothes, an ID, and a little money. You could feel her almost collapse when we told her to turn around and put her hands behind her back. She heard the sound of the cuffs opening up, that clicking sound. We put a jacket over her arms to hide them as she walked down her hallway, into the elevator, and then out into the lobby, in front of the doorman and her neighbors, people staring, but trying not to look as if they were. But people could still tell she was being arrested.

"Did you hear?" they would say as soon as she left the building. "She went out with cops, handcuffed."

I felt sorry for her as we walked through the lobby. Some crimes are so cruel and violent you hate the offender. Others are just stupid and desperate. In the car she recovered a little bit, tried going on the offensive. I wasn't bothered by it. In a strange way, I kind of admired her spirit.

"No one read me my Miranda rights," she said from the back of the car with handcuffs on.

"No, ma'am, you're right," I answered, from the passenger seat in front.

"Well, that's a violation of my rights."

"No, ma'am, it's not."

"Why not? You're supposed to read me my rights."

"Ma'am, no one has asked you any questions."

This silenced her. She leaned back and looked out the window. I could see a tear forming in the corner of her eye from the rearview window. What a sudden, radical change in the perspective of her life, looking out at the living city, the businesses, the traffic, people walking, restaurants, and knowing she was likely going to the county jail, a place she was completely unprepared for. It would be a brutal experience for her. Just a few minutes earlier she was drinking coffee on her deck over the river. I looked at her face in the mirror again. It was easy to read: *Why did I do it? Why? If I had only known. A quarter of a million. Will I go to prison?*

Now Madison Hobley was going to Area 2 in the back of a squad car. He was going as a witness. This was a septuple murder, with many more injured, the news everywhere. I could see him sitting in the backseat, looking out the window at the life going on around him. As he rode, Hobley was still conversing with the detectives. They knew what they were doing. It was during this ride that Hobley said to detectives that he had not seen his mistress, Angela McDaniel, since he had asked her to move out of their apartment earlier that winter so his wife and child could return, a request that infuriated McDaniel.

Lotito and Dwyer now had enough evidence and statements to begin hashing out the elements of their case. At the station, for example, they gathered more information about the fire. The narrative Hobley provided began falling apart. The description of how Hobley escaped the fire didn't hold up. The investigators told Lotito and Dwyer that Hobley could not have gone out into the hallway as he described. He would have been turned into ashes, they said. Equally important, Hobley's claim that the smoke was coming from the rear of the building on the second floor completely contradicted the evidence at the scene. The burn pattern, the one Hobley's lawyers would spend years contesting, showed the fire clearly came up the stairs near Hobley's apartment, right up to his apartment door. Hobley, the detectives realized, was not being truthful. There was another issue. The witnesses at the crime scene all commented that Hobley showed no emotion about losing his wife and child. Witnesses were also contradicting Hobley's statements about what he was wearing at the fire scene. The strange act of Hobley handing a bag of clothes without any prompting was starting to make sense. Hobley had told detectives he was wearing the same coat in the back of their car as he wore at the time of the fire. But now witnesses were coming forward, saying Hobley had been wearing a blue peacoat.

And it wasn't just the coat. At the scene of the fire, in the chaos of people jumping from windows and babies being tossed out, Hobley had spoken to several witnesses. Hobley had described to these witnesses an entirely different scenario of how he had come to escape, but not his wife and child. Hobley told these people that he had awakened his wife, but she had refused to go out of the building with him. With these anomalies in Hobley's narrative, the detectives read Hobley his rights and began to confront him about the contradictions. It was then that another contradiction in Hobley's statements emerged. During this next interview, after detectives had read Hobley his rights, Hobley stated he had spoken to his mistress, Angela McDaniel, much more recently than when he had first described in the back of the detectives' car. Hobley now told detectives he had spoken to her just a few days earlier. In this interview, Hobley still claimed McDaniel was the likely offender, and he warned the detectives that McDaniel had a violent brother, who was extremely dangerous, a statement that implicated the brother as a possible offender.

In this interview, Hobley once again modified his statement about the fire. This time, he said he awoke to the sound of a smoke detector and that he woke his wife and she walked to the apartment door with him, a door that fire investigators said would have been on fire, with smoke pouring into the apartment along with intense heat. Hobley told the detectives that he went down the back stairs after going out into the hallway but had been unable to get back in. He said his goal was to get his wife and child to jump from the window of their apartment. But there were no witnesses who ever saw Hobley go to the ground below his window and call up to them. Rather, he helped other people rescue victims but never went to his own window. What father and husband, the detectives wondered, could with a clear conscience leave his loved ones in a burning apartment and make no attempt to rescue them?

This failure to find any witnesses who observed Hobley attempting to rescue Anita and Philip taps into another aspect of Hobley's behavior that both the detectives and witnesses observed. Throughout all the detectives' conversations with Hobley, he remained utterly cold and distant about the fact that he had just lost his wife and child. There was no wailing, no sign of devastation that most people would express after such a tragic loss, particularly one that occurred in such a horrific manner. With all these emerging contradictions, the detectives asked Hobley if he would take a polygraph test. He agreed. In order to do so, the detectives would have to transport Hobley from the far South Side to police headquarters at Eleventh and State.

Dwyer and Lotito asked two other detectives to transport Hobley so that they could find Angela McDaniel and get a statement from her. Hobley provided Dywer and Lotito with information on how to track her down. They discovered McDaniel worked downtown, a short distance from police headquarters. But even as they began to make these arrangements, the credibility of Hobley's story suffered more crucial blows. Hobley had told detectives that he was working when the first fire in the building occurred on New Year's Eve, the one that did no harm. Dwyer and Lotito checked it out and discovered Hobley had not been working at the time.

They also learned that paramedics responded to the call at Hobley's mother's house around four a.m., a few hours after the fire. These paramedics came from a more distant fire station because so many other fire personnel were still tied up at the fire scene or at various hospitals. The detectives spoke to the paramedics. When they arrived, they told the detectives, Hobley told them he wanted some kind of sedative to calm down. They conducted basic tests, blood pressure, heart rate, et cetera. The paramedics told Hobley they couldn't give him any medication, but they could take him to St. Bernard Hospital. Hobley told the paramedics he would go but first he had to change his clothes. The paramedics indicated that Hobley was wearing a blue peacoat, just as the witnesses at the fire had described seeing him wearing. Paramedic Thomas Sullivan said he saw Hobley through a crack in the bedroom door on his hands and knees and clothes "flying around." Was this even more evidence that Hobley was trying to hide the original clothes he was wearing at the scene of the fire? Whoever set the fire carried gasoline into the building from some as yet unknown location and splashed the gasoline all over Hobley's door and on the floor outside of it, then down the stairs. Some gasoline surely spilled on the offender's clothes and hands.

Lotito and Dwyer went to the address of Angela McDaniel's grandparents, with whom she lived. They provided an alibi, saying Angela had been at home when the fire was set. They also described the tensions between McDaniel and Hobley, the fact that he was constantly calling her, but they would not put her on the phone. Next, the detectives went to her job downtown and met her on her lunch break outside the office building. Apprised of what Hobley had said about her, McDaniel denied that she had anything to do with the arson. McDaniel described the marital problems between Hobley and his wife. The tensions were so high, McDaniel told them, that Anita Hobley had stabbed Madison with a knife, and Madison had somehow secretly taken their child, Philip. She described how Hobley had left his wife and rented the apartment where Madison and Angela would live together on Eighty-Second Street. Eventually Hobley told McDaniel he had changed his mind and that he was going to move his wife and child into the apartment they shared. McDaniel was furious, particularly since she had put down some money for the apartment. She broke it off with Madison, but he continued to call her. Then McDaniel told the detectives about a meeting with Hobley five days before the arson. Hobley had insisted that they meet at a bar on the South Side. McDaniel told the detectives that Hobley was completely distraught and confused about the situation. On the one hand, he wanted to be with McDaniel. On the other, he could not abide by anyone being with his wife. Hobley suggested that the four of them live together, at which time McDaniel became extremely angry. Hobley's absurd suggestion that the two women could live in the same household was a sign of how unraveled he was becoming. McDaniel issued an ultimatum. Pick one of us. Hobley, she said, stated that he could not bear to have another man raise his son. Then McDaniel again denied to the detectives that she had anything to do with either fire at the building, the one on New Year's Eve or the one that had just claimed seven lives. Her alibi mirrored what her grandparents said. McDaniel agreed to go back to headquarters with the detectives and take a polygraph, which she passed.

It was at this stage of the investigation that Lotito and Dwyer obtained a key witness. After they interviewed McDaniel, they received a call from two other detectives, who told them they had discovered a man who owned the gas station near Hobley's apartment. His name was Kenneth Stewart. Stewart told these detectives that he had sold gasoline to a man carrying a gas can shortly before the fire. He told detectives that the man matched the description of Hobley. Stewart was being brought to police headquarters for a lineup, the detectives were told.

Then another key witness stepped forward, probably one of the most compelling witnesses in the whole investigation. It was a rookie Chicago police officer named Glenn Evans. Evans told detectives that he and his partner were assigned a call of criminal damage to property on November 29, 1986, about six weeks before the fatal arson. The complainant, Patricia Phiefer, had called police because someone had thrown a brick through the window of her apartment. Phiefer told Evans and his partner she believed that the offender was Madison Hobley. Phiefer suspected Hobley because Phiefer had experienced his violent outbursts first-hand. Phiefer was friends with Anita Hobley and had taken Anita and her son, Philip, into her home when Anita left Hobley after finding out about his affair with McDaniel. Hobley had been calling Phiefer, demanding to speak to his wife, but she would not let him. As Phiefer was telling this to Evans and his partner, the phone rang. Phiefer said it was probably Hobley again. She asked the officers to listen to the call on another phone. Evans did so, picking up the phone and listening in. In the conversation, Evans heard Hobley admit to breaking the window and threaten to set Phiefer's building on fire.

Alarmed at Hobley's threat, Evans and his partner completed the case report on the criminal damage, citing in the narrative the fact that they overheard Hobley make threats of committing an arson. For detectives Lotito and Dwyer, this was a kind of nail in the coffin. They had Hobley on several lies, his suspicious behavior, and conflicting statements, and now a fellow officer stepped forward and told them there was a case report listing arson threats made by Hobley six weeks earlier. With the case report brought forth by Evans, the detectives had established Hobley as a prime suspect.

Hobley went for the polygraph. At the end of it, Detective Garrity looked at the results and told Hobley he didn't think Hobley was telling the truth. Hobley broke down and told Garrity that he had been lying. He had set the fire. Hobley said he had walked to a nearby gas station, bought the gas, walked back to the apartment, spread the gas outside the apartment and down the front stairs and landings, then ignited it with a match. Hobley told Garrity he threw the gas can down the hallway of the second floor. By the time Garrity heard this confession from Hobley, detectives had already obtained the witness from the gas station, the owner Kenneth Stewart, who corroborated Hobley's statement about walking to the gas station and filling the can with gas.

The investigation pressed on.

Informed by Garrity of this initial confession , Lotito and Dwyer brought him back to an interview room. They confronted Hobley with what they had: the statements by McDaniel, the discovery of new witnesses refuting Hobley's story, the gas station attendant who witnessed Hobley buy the gas, the fact that this witness was on his way to the station to view Hobley in a lineup, and then the forensic evidence that rejected the whole notion that Hobley walked out of the apartment after the fire had been ignited. Hobley hung his head and repeated what he had said to Detective Garrity.

"I just couldn't handle Anita anymore," Hobley said about his wife. "It's not that Angela's any better looking or nothing. She's just together. She's where I want to be in my future."

At this point, Hobley also admitted he had lied about what clothes he was wearing, just as all the witnesses had said. Now the bath and the changing of the clothes before leaving with the paramedics were making more sense to the detectives. At the lineup, the owner of the gas station, Kenneth Stewart, said Hobley looked like the guy he saw purchasing the gas shortly before the fire. Right after they scheduled the lineup, the commanding officer told two detectives to go back to Hobley's apartment building and look for the gas can he said he had thrown down the hallway. The detectives did, in fact, find a gas can in a second-floor apartment, which they took possession of, inventoried, and sent to the laboratory to look for fingerprints.

Up to this point in their investigation, Hobley had cooperated fully with the detectives. They had read him his rights, confronted him with the emerging contradictions of his story and evidence of his guilt. He failed the lie detector and confessed, then confessed again. The detectives were with Hobley in an interview room after he confessed when an attorney, Steven Stern, suddenly appeared. Stern was Hobley's cousin. Both Lotito and Dwyer were surprised that Stern was able to come into the back of the station without the detectives being alerted. Normally, an attorney was told to wait, and a cop at the desk would go back and alert the detectives that a lawyer had arrived. A detective would then come to the desk and escort the attorney to his client. After Stern had wandered back into the station to the interview rooms, he had been able to look through a one-way mirror and see the detectives interviewing Hobley without the detectives knowing.

Angry that Stern had just been allowed into the back of the station without an escort or without the detectives being notified, Dwyer and Lotito met with Stern outside the room. Stern said he was Hobley's attorney. Dwyer asked for a card and said he would ask Hobley if Stern was indeed Hobley's attorney. Stern agreed. Inside the room, Hobley told Dwyer that, yes, Stern was his lawyer. The detectives then left Stern alone with Hobley for about ten minutes. Stern emerged from the room with the door opened so that Hobley could see him, but now Stern's demeanor was completely changed. Stern spoke aggressively and condescendingly to Dwyer and Lotito. He told the detectives that he didn't want anyone else talking to his client. It was clear to the detectives that Stern was putting on a show for Hobley. Dwyer was furious with Stern. He told Stern to step away from the door and closed it. Dwyer pointed out to Stern that he could interview Hobley all he wanted, as long as Hobley agreed to it, and that Stern could not command the detectives about how to do their job. He also pointed out that up until that moment after Hobley had spoken to Stern, Hobley had been completely cooperative and had already confessed. Stern then told the detectives that Hobley had told him he had been abused. Stern said Hobley was now claiming he was punched and kicked and had a plastic bag placed over his head. The detectives were furious and confronted Stern over the validity of these claims.

Here it is important to place this interaction between Stern and the detectives in context. The Hobley arson was in 1987, five years after the Andrew Wilson murders of Fahey and O'Brien, but long enough that the mythology about Burge and his men had begun. This claim of being abused was the only argument left to suspects who had confessed, suspects for whom there was a massive amount of evidence against them.

Dwyer pointed out that when Stern had been watching them interview Hobley from outside the room through the one-way mirror, the detectives didn't even know he was there. The detectives pointed out that Stern could see they weren't coercing Hobley in any way. Dwyer told Stern he was making these allegations of abuse because his client had already confessed and because Stern lacked the professional skill and knowledge to develop any other kind of defense other than false allegations. Dwyer pointed out the absence of marks on Hobley. So angry was Dwyer that he told Stern he would get him listed as a witness for the defense in the trial and make Stern admit under oath that he had not seen any abuse, something Dwyer eventually did.

The state's attorney, the prosecutor, arrived on scene. When the prosecutor walked into the room where Hobley was being held, Hobley was twisting and wrenching his handcuffs, which caused some abrasions on his wrists. It is a common reaction for people when they realize they are being charged with murder, charged with an offense that could get them the death penalty, to become somewhat hysterical. After having met with his attorney, Hobley was now not cooperating. He refused to talk to the prosecutor. Word spread that the police had a suspect. The media gathered for the perp walk. On the way out of the building, Hobley asked the detectives if he could speak to the media. Lotito and Dwyer reminded him that he had just refused to talk to the prosecutor. The detectives asked him why he now wanted to talk.

"No matter what I done, man, I don't want to die, and I don't want their people going by messing with my family," Hobley responded.

Then Hobley called out to the media as he walked past them.

"They got the wrong man. I didn't do it."

The detectives already believed they had a rock-solid

case, but the following day it got even better. Another witness, Andre Council, who had been at the gas station, contacted Area 2 detectives. Council told the detectives that he had stopped the night of the fire at the gas station owned by Kenneth Stewart. They were friends. Council often worked at the station, fixing flat tires and pumping gas. That night he came to the station to buy fifty cents' worth of gas, just enough to get home. While he was at the pump, he observed Madison Hobley approach and fill a gas can, just as Stewart had described. While filling it, Hobley spilled some of the gas on Council's truck. Council stared at Hobley, expecting an apology, but Hobley just turned around and walked back in the direction he came from, the direction of the crime scene, carrying the gas can.

While Council was still at the gas station, he heard fire engines approaching on Cottage Grove. He saw them turn eastbound toward the fire and his own residence. He went home to make sure his building wasn't on fire. After making sure it wasn't, he and several of his relatives walked over to the scene of the fire. There, he observed Hobley standing in front of the building and talking to a man and a woman. Council heard Hobley say that his wife and baby were still in the building. He listened to Hobley's conversation carefully. Hobley caught Council's attention because, unlike any other people on the scene, Hobley displayed no emotion. Hobley, Council said, just as the other witnesses had told detectives, made no attempt to rescue his wife or child or even communicate with them. Hobley never shouted up to the window of his apartment. Council then watched Hobley walk away from the scene. Council's statement about Hobley's bizarre behavior mirrored others' descriptions. Council went home. Watching the news later on, he saw Hobley being escorted by the police during Hobley's perp walk. He recognized him instantly, from both the gas station and the crime scene. Council called the police. Council also spoke to his friend Kenneth Stewart. Stewart informed Council that he had tentatively identified Hobley at a lineup. Stewart told Council he was fearful of ratting on anyone and figured Hobley would only get a few years, but after speaking with Council, he realized the gravity of the crime. Council said that in his conversations with Stewart, Stewart confided that he was more certain that Hobley was the man who bought the gas than Stewart had originally stated to the police and prosecutor at the lineup. Council's witness statement was the final overwhelming piece of evidence in the case. His statement matched Kenneth Stewart's and Hobley's own confession. Hobley had been standing right next to Council filling the gas can, then Council had seen Hobley at the crime scene.

The following day, based on all of the witness statements about what clothes Hobley was wearing and by his own confession that he had lied about what he was wearing, detectives obtained a search warrant for Hobley's mother's apartment. They searched it, but could not find the clothes or any other evidence. Where had they gone?

Hobley was tried for the seven murders and convicted. The jury called for the death penalty. Hobley was on death row at the same time and in the same prison as Anthony Porter. In 1999 he watched Porter walk free, getting out of a double murder. All the death row inmates saw this. Hobley pressed his case that he too was innocent, and in 2003 he also walked out of prison. Hobley's release was different from Porter's in that Hobley's was obtained from a governor's pardon, for Hobley's attorneys had failed to sway any jury, judge, or court that he was innocent. They all bolstered his conviction. Hobley's release, therefore, set a precedent. It was the first time a man was pardoned off death row without any new evidence, simply by the whim of a governor who declared he was innocent. At the time of his pardon, Governor George Ryan cited the Porter case as central motive in his reconsideration of the Hobley case. Ryan was also facing his own twenty-one count indictment for corruption in a pay-to-play scandal from when Ryan was secretary of state. And it wasn't just Hobley whom Ryan freed. At the same time Hobley was pardoned, three other convicted killers were also released.

The detectives believed Hobley was guilty. So did the prosecutors, the jury, and the judge. Hobley had lost his appeals. All the legal proceedings fingered him for the murders. Yet he walked free. In his release, certainly a revolution had taken shape in the city. If the Porter exoneration crumbled under the weight of renewed scrutiny, then I believed others would crumble, including the Hobley exoneration, and I was willing to gamble everything on this belief, both as a cop and a writer, absolutely everything. But it required some official declaration by a leader of one of Chicago's corrupt institutions—institutions that let this travesty unfold to begin with. This is why in the fall of 2014 I was so anxious waiting for

Alvarez to make a statement about the Porter case, about whether she would let Simon out of prison. Would Alvarez stand up? Would she change the orthodox history? And if she did, would anyone in the city tie the Porter case to the Hobley arson? That would mean that a central case used in the Burge mythology was also proven false.

Sitting at my desk in 2014 with the transcripts and records of both the Porter and Hobley cases stacked about my apartment, these were the thoughts running through my mind. Would Alvarez release Simon from prison? I got up and walked outside my condo to the shore of Lake Michigan, grateful that a breeze had now kicked up and there were white clouds moving in from the eastern horizon, blotting out the sun and dropping the temperature somewhat. I walked into the water about shin deep, a cooling chill, and saw some people pull up with children and beach toys. *What the hell*, I decided, and walked out into deeper water until I had to swim. Looking back onshore, I could see the lifeguard walking toward me from the other end of the beach. She would demand that I come closer to shore, that I was too far out, but for a least a few minutes now I pretended I could not hear her. Past the rocks offshore, the waves were regular, picking me up and setting me down, like some benevolent fatefulness. I let them do so, until I heard an angry voice back onshore. I turned around in the water, seeing the lifeguard flailing her arms at me, demanding that I come in. I didn't want to, but, being a cop and all, I had to.

Chapter 10

IVORY TOWERS

It was the smell of popcorn that brought back so many memories. It hit me as soon as I opened the door to the underground bar, Streeter's, on Chicago Avenue. It had been more than five years since I had been inside it. This was the regular bar for many of us after work during the years I worked as a doorman. After lifting hundreds of bags on a hot summer day at the Allerton Hotel, Jeff, the bell captain, and I would retreat here. We would drink three beers before we even started chatting, the beer making us boozy quickly because of our fatigue. We would watch sports on the television and talk about the job, but in the end we usually ended up talking about Chicago, for Jeff had spent three decades in the city and was one of the most eloquent people I had ever met, certainly one of the most streetwise. His stories about growing up a black man on a farm in the Deep South, then making his way to Chicago, were enthralling, hilarious, and tragic. I remember him telling me about the summer day he was working in the fields with his uncle. He was so hot and so exhausted, he had to pause. A lifetime of doing such work was too much for him. He looked at his uncle and said, "I can't do this anymore." A week later he was on a train headed for the city.

Jeff had started out at the Allerton as a part-time bellman on midnights, but his encyclopedic knowledge of the city's geography, garnered from his years of hustling and living the high life, made him too valuable to remain in such an obscure position. His knowledge, gift of gab, and street smarts made him one of the highest money earners in the hotel. He cultivated relationships with every maître d', every manager, and every theater owner in the city, and he turned these relationships into generous tips. I would stand dumbfounded in the lobby on a busy Sunday morning as a line of grateful guests about to check out would hand him fives and tens for his services. After it slowed down, he would come out to the front of the hotel where I was standing, pull out his wad of cash as if he were rearranging the bills, but he was really taunting me with how much he made. Jeff and I were such good friends, we spoke to each other only in insults at the beginning and end of every conversation.

"You turning tricks again?" I would ask.

"No. I'm not interested in horning in on your business," Jeff responded without looking up, still arranging bills.

"You need to borrow a few bucks, kid?" he asked.

"No, I'm good. I had a good day."

"You mean you made twenty bucks today? You can get a hamburger and a forty-ouncer tonight and watch the ball-

game in your little apartment. That's fantastic. I'm happy
for you."

"Fuck you."

"No, no, no. Fuck you."

It was Jeff's lectures at the bar that I found most fascinating,
because Jeff had run with some of the biggest gangsters in
the city. He had been a prominent drug dealer before his
cocaine habit had reduced him to near homelessness and he
was forced to start over, getting a lowly part-time job at the
Allerton on midnights. Even at the hotel, I knew he was still
moving some weed, because employees from every department in the hotel suddenly needed to talk to him privately
on payday, and he was always flush with cash, always, even
more cash than could be earned from tips. Jeff worked inside,
near the desk, but when things slowed down, he wandered to
the front and we chatted in between check-ins. Jeff, too, had
taught me the art of being a doorman, his mentoring tripling
my daily income, so that I eventually walked home every
night with a wad of ones, fives, tens, and twenties almost as
large as his. Jeff always walked home carrying a pistol, which
he casually shoved down his waistband in the locker room
before heading home, as routinely as he put on his coat.

"Preib," he told me one day just a few months after I had
begun working at the hotel, both of us standing in front of
the hotel after I loaded up a cab for an O'Hare run, "there's
too much money flowing out of this corner without you
getting a taste. That's your cabstand and you're not getting
anything out of it."

"Well, what the fuck do you want me to do about it?" I said. "They want a cab, I get them a cab."

Jeff looked at me with disgust, shook his head, then walked back into the hotel. I knew I was in for some humiliation. A day or so later, a guest walked up to both of us standing outside the hotel and asked about cab fare to the airport. Before I could answer, Jeff interrupted me.

"I tell you what, sir. You want a ride to the airport, I'll have a Lincoln Town Car waiting for you, flat rate of twenty-five dollars to the airport, about the same as a cab, few dollars more maybe. It's clean, roomy, and the driver is a professional and speaks English," Jeff said.

"Would you?" the guest said.

"I most certainly will."

Jeff jotted down the guest's information, then handed him a slip with the name of a driver on it. He went inside and called a driver and booked it. Later that day, Jeff was again waiting outside when the Lincoln Town Car pulled up. The driver waved. Jeff waved back indicating he wanted the driver to get out.

"This is a friend of mine," he told the driver, Juan. "He's the new doorman here. He'll be giving you some rides to the airport, same as me."

The driver nodded, shook my hand, and gave me his card. A minute later, the guest came out. I went to grab his luggage to load him up, in the hopes of maybe getting some tip out of it, but Jeff blocked me with his arm.

"Yes, sir," he told the guest. "This is Juan. He'll be your driver." Jeff then grabbed the man's luggage before the guy could say anything. Jeff walked to the back of the car where

Juan was waiting. Out of the view of the guest, Juan handed Jeff a five-dollar bill, Jeff's cut for booking the ride. Then Jeff walked over to the door of the Town Car and held it open. He took another five-dollar bill from the guest as the guest got in the car, thanking Jeff profusely. Jeff, looking at me, pulled out his wad of cash and placed the two five-dollar bills on top.

"You see how that's done," Jeff said to me, laughing. "You can do that all day long out here. Every car that goes to O'Hare should be at least five bucks for you. If not, you are not doing your job."

I looked out on the street, silent.

"Just remember, kid. I taught you everything you know, but not everything I know."

"Fuck you," I said.

"No, fuck you," he said, walking away, laughing.

From that day on, I had Town Car after Town Car taking guests to the airport, sometimes fifteen in a day. With Jeff's mentoring, I was running all kinds of scams from the hotel. Jeff told me I had to "educate" people to tip me. When I was getting cabs for people on a rainy night and they got into the cab without tipping, people behind them would often think it was okay not to tip either. Jeff taught me to always have a one-dollar bill fingered in my hand, so that even if they didn't tip, I pretended they did. I pulled out the dollar bill and put it in my pocket in front of the crowd waiting for a taxi, as if the guest had just handed it to me as he got in the cab. I said thank you loudly so everyone could hear. It worked like a charm. Everyone in line pulled out a dollar and gave it to me. When people were asking all kinds of questions about where to eat, Jeff would walk up to me, hand me a ten-dollar bill, and say, "This is from those people you got into that Italian restaurant yesterday." The people now asking so many questions would pull out a ten and also hand it over.

Education.

Restaurant managers gave us five dollars for every guest we sent there. Soon, we sent so many guests to restaurants that we began eating free all over the city. Jeff took his wife. I came with my girlfriend. The managers would not let us order off the menu, just bringing us dishes, one after the other.

Summer nights after there were few or no check-ins left, Jeff would relieve me on the door. It was a signal. I headed out to the liquor store a block away, buying a six-pack of good beer. I took it to the basement of the old hotel, put it in a wine container, then added ice on top. Covering it with a napkin, I went back to the elevator, pushed the button for the lower lobby at street level. When the door opened, I'd hold it open with my foot until Jeff looked toward me, then wave to him.

"What took you so long? Are you blind or did you see a tranny again?" I would say as Jeff came into the elevator.

"I did. He looked just like you," Jeff would say as he got on the elevator. Jeff would hit the button for the top, the twenty-fourth floor. There, we'd go down the hallway to the fire escape door, brace it open with the pack of beer, and sit down on the fire escape. I would pass one beer to Jeff. We'd look out at the city, talking shit and drinking. We could see everything: the lake, Michigan Avenue, all the neighborhoods spread out before us. After an hour or so, we'd head off to Streeter's, a late night of drinking ahead of us.

Now I walked into the bar, about the same age as Jeff was when we had met. I limped a little from a stiff back, three surgeries behind me now, and Jeff was dead. He overdosed on cocaine, still working at the hotel years after I had left. He was living in a transient hotel on Wells Street, snorting coke and smoking weed all morning with some friends when his asthma began to bother him. His wife had kicked him out of their home on the West Side, fed up with his addiction. Jeff still went to church with her on Sundays, but this day he called her and said he couldn't make it because of an asthma attack. A little while later, standing in the hallway, he could barely breathe and whispered loud enough for his friends to hear, "Heavenly Father, forgive me my sins," and he died. I drove down to Chicago from Michigan in a blizzard to attend the funeral. I had never been to a black Baptist funeral. I spoke at the funeral, arguing that in many ways Jeff was one of the most religious men I had ever met, that whenever he talked about Christ, he stressed that Christ went out into the world. Jeff liked this image of Christ more than the one in churches and ceremonies. Later I learned that Jeff's friends had gone back into his hotel room after the ambulance rushed him away and stole his pistol, his drugs, and his money.

I sidled up to the bar at Streeter's, seeing no faces that I remembered among the workers or regulars. No longer drinking beer, I went straight to the hard stuff, rye whiskey.

After the first few sips, I could hear Jeff's voice again. I looked around. It was a place I spent so much of my youth. It was difficult not to conclude that I had wasted much of my life in shitty jobs, then at bars. Nevertheless, I found being back on the stool comforting, familiar, and cozy. I didn't want to leave. I didn't want to face the fact that I would soon have to abandon this comfort and familiarity to go to Loyola University around the corner. Tonight I was scheduled to lead my first presentation about corruption in the wrongful conviction movement. A professor in the criminal justice department was a former police commander. He had read my book, liked it, and fought to hold a panel discussion about it. As soon as he announced the discussion, many other professors protested, but the professor fought them off. I had invited Charles Salvatore, one of the lead detectives in the Porter case, and Rick Beuke, one of Burge's lawyers, to be part of the discussion. Invitations to prominent wrongful conviction attorneys and activists went unanswered, so we would be presenting our story about Alstory Simon being innocent and possibly released from prison any day. Here was one of my first opportunities to present our argument about the Porter case.

It wasn't the first time I had spoken at Loyola. When my first book came out about five years earlier, I was invited to speak in front of a humanities class. Once again I had come to Streeter's beforehand and drunk too much whiskey. I was so ashamed of myself, being lit up in front of a bunch of kids, though I don't think any of them realized it. As soon as I walked into the class, sat down at a desk positioned slightly higher than the students', like a podium, and looked out across the room, I knew why I wanted to be drunk. There was a sea of faces looking at me with a countenance of complete apathy. It was clear few of them wanted to be there. I was to tell them about a book I had spent years writing, talk to them about what authors were my favorite and why, but most of them couldn't care less. I hated it. It was a required class in the pursuit of a degree, so they showed up because they had to. There are few things more depressing than talking about something you feel passionate about to indifferent, even hostile, people. To my great relief, there were a few kids who asked some really good questions and seemed interested, and a meager discussion flowed. But when I walked out into the night air afterward, I felt so relieved to be out of there and so guilty for appearing in front of kids drunk.

And yet, here at Streeter's again before another presentation at Loyola, I ordered a third whiskey, sipped it. My relationship with Loyola went back even further, to my first years in the city as a doorman. I signed up at the university to take one class a semester, Latin. I had taken classical Greek as an undergrad. Now I wanted to round it out a little, initiate some kind of imaginative life by reading and studying the classics rather than just be a working stiff day after day. And so in the mornings I arose, went to a café near my apartment in Rogers Park, studied for several hours, went to Latin class, came home, and got ready for my doorman job working with Jeff. At work, I kept notecards in the pocket of my uniform with Latin noun and verb forms, repeating them over and over as I paced in front of the hotel looking to make some tips. Thinking about these days in Streeter's, I smiled, for they were among the happiest of my life.

But then school administrators kept telling me I had to declare a major, become part of a program, and then, well, I faded away again, dropping out of Latin in the fourth semester and getting collection letters from the university for the tuition until I went on a payment plan. Every week I paid an installment at the bursar's office. Each time I walked into the building now I was a stranger, no longer enrolled. Another failed undertaking, another furtive flight to nowhere. I arrived in my doorman uniform at the downtown campus one afternoon to pay off the last ninety dollars and got into an argument with the lady, who said I owed fifty more.

Here I was now, twenty years later, the drunken prodigal son returning to Loyola to tell everyone, everyone at the university, that they had it all wrong, all wrong, you see. There is a revolution under way. It's all around us. Look. Look at this court case. I took another sip, surprised that the glass was empty so soon, so I nodded at the bartender when he looked at me from the other end of the bar. I lifted the glass sideways for a moment, so that a little whiskey formed in the corner, and I lifted it to my lips, and I kissed it.

I traced the history of our love affair. It was such a long path in my life to finding rye whiskey. Most people I knew when I was young drank Scotch whisky, but I hated the peat taste. Then I read an article about Irish whiskey, tried it, and had a revelation, as if I finally felt a connection to my vague ancestors, or at least some of them. I read some more about whiskeys, then learned that bourbon was a native form of it.

Talk about finding a home, feeling as if you finally belonged. Cooked up in the mountains of Kentucky and Tennessee. I thought I had arrived. It was so natural, so dignified. I drank it for about a year when things got even better. Someone told me about Manhattans made with rye whiskey. I read that rye and Manhattans, along with old-fashioneds, were once one of the most common drinks before Prohibition but had never fully recovered in popularity after alcohol became legal again. So I tried a rye whiskey one day in a Manhattan. Now I didn't have to go to Kentucky, didn't even have to leave my condo or the city. Rye had an earthy taste, as if it came right from the soil underneath me. It was strong, but not pretentious, had no airs whatsoever. It could be made in fancy distilleries or a still in the woods. But rye was more powerful than anything else. It took you to places you had only imagined, but the following day it sent a bill, and I knew that tomorrow, no matter what happened at Loyola, I would have to pay it.

I turned away from this thought, reconfiguring myself on the bar stool at the same time. Loyola went further back than even the Latin class, to a past I could not make out clearly, and not just because I was drunk. My father had gone to school there after serving in World War II. Walking about the university, I felt even more powerfully that I lived in his shadow. He had just come back from serving in the war when he attended the school. I, on the other hand, was a doorman downtown. My mother went to Mundelein College next door. There were wedding pictures taken on the steps of her school. Trying to look so far backward, my thoughts started faltering. I looked up at one of the television screens and saw two where there should be one. I knew that slurring my words could not be far behind. Not good, prodigal son, to be seeing double before you give a presentation at a university. Time to put on the brakes, or was it too late? I felt myself sinking now, sinking quickly. Rick hadn't met me here as planned. Neither had Chuck. Would I face this alone? Would I arrive to tell everyone that it was just me, slurring my words, my shirt untucked? Would I drop my papers, stumble, fall to the floor, and have to be helped up? Would I throw up on myself?

Just then I felt a hand on my shoulder. I turned to Rick, one of the best defense attorneys in the city, with his wife. I steadied. We could handle this. They ordered a round. I'd just sip one more. Charles showed up a little while later. Police stories broke out, then it was time to head over.

The room was well lit, disorienting. There was a decent crowd, spread out around the room. I stared out from the table in front. I faltered a little at first, almost slurring my words. I began with the announcement that an innocent man was in prison and how unusual it was that I, a cop, was fighting for his release. Feeling more comfortable, I described the murder itself in Washington Park. The attendees were listening to me, following what I was saying. There were some academics in the crowd, some cops, some students. Rick and Charles took my cues to tell their side of the story. Eventually, someone asked if I thought Anita Alvarez was going to let Simon out of prison.

"I really don't know," I said. "I'm of two minds about it." Afterward, a group of us, mostly retired cops, wandered back to Streeter's.

Chapter 11

ON THE ROAD AGAIN

I was driving east on a California road whose name I did not know, mountains all around me. Originally, I had headed west, hoping to make it to the Pacific coast, but the road came to an abrupt end, some sixty miles or so since I had gotten on it. Now I had no choice but to go back the way I had come. The road was narrow, barely able to fit two cars passing each other, and there were no guardrails protecting a driver from the steep valleys below. I had been drinking coffee and water as I switched back and forth on the winding path, and now I needed to piss, but there was nowhere safe to pull over. As I caught glimpses of the valleys and peaks of mountains, I concluded that most people would be intoxicated by such a landscape, but not me. I was lost again, far from Chicago. I wasn't sure if I should return all the way back east to Interstate 5 or wait for someone to come along, wave them down, and ask for guidance, for a possible route I had missed.

Take it easy, you fucking pussy, I told myself. *Calm the fuck down. You're a fucking cop for Christ's sake.* As I said this to myself, I was also casting glimpses into the lush trees and bushes on the side of the road, wondering if there were bears or mountain lions in them. This rumination added to my anxiety about stopping to piss. I had this image of a driver rounding the curve and seeing a large bear gnawing at my innards in the middle of the road, too late to help me. In my absurd situation, switching back and forth on the mountain road, I couldn't help but take stock of how I had arrived in the mountains of California, completely lost, again.

Cook County Prosecutor Alvarez released Alstory Simon the day after my presentation at Loyola. I was still hung over and in bed when I got the phone call early in the morning from Alstory Simon in prison. In the course of my researching and writing about his case, we had come to speak on the phone almost every day.

"Hey, Marty," I heard him say, the familiar shouts of other inmates in the background. "Something is going on. They came to my cell with some paperwork they wanted me to sign, some stuff about my property."

"Do you think this is it, Al?" I asked.

"Yeah, I do."

"Well, that's fucking fantastic. I don't believe it. Congratulations. I didn't think we'd ever get this done. Do your thing. I'll talk to you later, when you are on the outside," I said.

"Okay, I will. Thanks for everything," he said.

When I hung up, I looked at my phone again. There were several messages, all, it turned out, telling me Al would be getting out that day. The media had caught on. One message said that Alvarez had scheduled a press conference for that afternoon at her office downtown. I went to my contacts and hit Bill Crawford's name.

"You heard?" I said.

"Yeah," he said.

"You going down to the press conference?"

"Yes. Can't miss that."

"Me too. I'll meet you there."

Bill Crawford was a retired *Tribune* journalist who had first broken the Porter story. We had now become a team in researching the case in hopes of getting Simon out. Bill had researched it using public records, particularly the court records. I tracked down Charles Salvatore, a detective who had worked the case. Salvatore opened the door for me to interview other detectives from this same era who had been accused of framing innocent men, including, eventually, Jon Burge. It had been a long road for all of us, beginning with our initial doubt about these exonerations to the freeing of Alstory Simon from prison. Our doubt extended beyond just the Porter case. After talking to so many detectives from this era, we had come to believe that many of the exonerations were equally suspicious. It was our hope that the Porter case would lead to a review of others, in particular the Hobley arson. For this reason, Bill and I were a kind of threat to Alvarez at her press conference, for Alvarez would not want to open up the door that an entire era in the city may be

false, an era in which Alvarez was a key player. Alvarez probably knew that we would ask questions she didn't want to
answer, especially if she did not declare Simon innocent, for
we believed he was innocent, believed we had proved it from
the research that fed our own writing.

How, we wondered before the press conference, would
Alvarez portray the decision by her predecessor, Dick
Devine, to release Porter and take Simon into custody in
1999? How would she gloss over the internal fighting that
took place in the prosecutor's office over that very question?
This period in the prosecutor's office cast a dark shadow. The
infighting there suggested that from the very moment
Alstory Simon confessed to the murders, prosecutors
doubted the story. Was this a sign that Alvarez covered up
the corruption in the Porter exoneration until people like Bill
and I had created so much media hoopla about it she could
no longer deny it? Now she was going to stand before the
press, portraying herself as a crusader for law and justice by
taking up the Simon case again. Would Alvarez go easy on
her predecessor, Dick Devine, or blast him for releasing
Porter? How would she explain that she let Simon languish
in prison for almost a decade before she took up his case?
Again, would she declare Simon innocent?

These questions were important not only to get Alstory
Simon, an innocent man, out of prison but to address what
the police went through in the wrongful conviction process.
Much of my life the last five years had been spent listening to
retired detectives talk about how false allegations of abuse
had ruined their lives and reputations. Their careers had
been destroyed and they had spent their retirement fighting

one allegation after another, dragged into yet another deposition by a collection of attorneys hell-bent on using the system against them. Always hanging over them was the fate of Jon Burge, sentenced to four and half years in federal prison. All these detectives wondered if they would end up there as well, even on cases that had withstood one legal inquiry after another, like the Hobley case.

I reviewed the narrative I had formed over this period of Chicago's history, so contrary to what was deemed official. Devine's decision to free Porter and to convict Simon in 1999 was the key victory for the wrongful conviction movement that initiated the full-fledged war on the Chicago Police Department. But our narrative, now given new life with Simon's release from prison, made the media as nervous as it did Alvarez. Gathering at the press conference were journalists who had covered the Porter story since 1999, now confronted with the fact that one of the most sensational stories in their era may be a complete fraud. A core group of them had played a central role in covering the Porter exoneration, journalists who had echoed David Protess's theories without checking the simplest facts. How many other cases had they gotten wrong? They had argued that the exonerations were interconnected, part of a pattern of police misconduct, but now a pattern of false exonerations was taking shape, one that they had helped create. The Hobley case loomed right after the Porter exoneration, for Governor Ryan cited the Porter exoneration in a speech announcing the release of Hobley and four other men as a key reason for letting these convicted killers out of prison in 2003:

I never intended to be an activist on this issue. I
watched in surprise as freed death row inmate
Anthony Porter was released from jail. A free man, he
ran into the arms of Northwestern University
Professor Dave Protess who poured his heart and soul
into proving Porter's innocence with his journalism
students. He was 48 hours away from being wheeled
into the execution chamber where the state would kill
him. It would all be so antiseptic and most of us
would not have even paused, except that Anthony
Porter was innocent of the double murder for which
he had been condemned to die.

If it weren't for the Porter case, Hobley would quite likely
never have gotten out, and now the Porter case was
unraveling.

And there was something even darker haunting the press
conference and the journalists who had worked in the era of
these exonerations. The Porter case was tied to the
mythology about Jon Burge and his men. After Hobley was
set free from death row by Ryan in 2003, he filed a lawsuit.
Burge was to be deposed in the course of that lawsuit. When
asked about abusing suspects in written interrogatories,
Burge denied it. This denial eventually became the basis of
perjury and obstruction of justice charges against Burge by
federal prosecutors, the wrongful conviction activists finally
getting the criminal conviction of Burge they had always
sought. Burge's criminal conviction arising from his statements in the Hobley case made the mythology about him

orthodox history. But as the Porter exoneration fell apart, the Hobley exoneration was also in danger. What would happen if the Hobley innocence narrative fell apart as the Porter narrative had? Hobley's exoneration, after all, was made without any new evidence of his innocence. What would happen if it was proven that Burge had been convicted based upon the false exoneration of a mass murderer? The villain upon whom the media's entire wrongful conviction mythology was based, the vilification of the police that they had been pushing since the 1968 riots at the Democratic Convention, would receive a mortal wound. That was the tension in the city with the release of Simon.

There were, to me, already signs of a guilty conscience in the media. None of them would talk to Bill, even though he had won the Pulitzer Prize and had retired from the *Tribune* after twenty-six years. He had uncovered the corruption in the Porter case and detailed it in a brilliant article he sent around to the press, not one of which ever took up his arguments. And yet now the prosecutor was setting Simon free, just as Bill had argued in that article that she should. It was a huge victory for his journalistic efforts, but no one even walked up to him. A few journalists nodded discreetly at me, particularly those I had fed stories over the years or provided with background information, but none of them would put us on the record. As Bill and I stood outside, Alvarez's spokesperson came down and said the media could come up. This moment should have been a triumphant walk for Bill and me, but we felt like strangers in a foreign, hostile land, and we were. I felt like a radical in the early days of a movement, walking amidst my enemies. I moved myself into the center of the group, worried that one of Alvarez's attorneys would claim I wasn't an official media member and kick me out. As a cop, I couldn't put up a fuss, lest they have me arrested or make a complaint to the department. No one said anything. We took our seats in the conference room, Bill and I sitting together.

Alvarez swooped into the crowded conference room with several other attorneys. She looked so nervous as she began reading her statement, I wasn't sure she would get through it. Her voice seemed on the verge of breaking. She announced that earlier that day she had released Simon after a year-long review. She did so because of evidence that Protess and Ciolino violated Simon's constitutional rights. This was the first declaration by an official body that the Northwestern professor's role in the Porter case was unethical. Later in her statement, Alvarez admitted that if the statute of limitations had not expired, she would have considered criminal charges against Ciolino and Protess. Why, then, we immediately asked ourselves, did she take so long in her investigation that she let the statute of limitations expire? Nevertheless, this was a statement about the Porter case that Bill and I had long coveted. But, to our dismay, Alvarez refused to declare Simon innocent. She said there were people on both sides of the issue making different claims. It was a big shrug of the shoulders. She copped out, an archetypical Chicago public official.

The time for questions came, and Bill pounced, immediately asking about the conduct of her predecessor, Dick Devine, who convicted Simon. As he did so, one of Alvarez's attorneys leaned in to her ear and whispered. Bill and I both felt he was telling Alvarez who we were. Alvarez nodded, then turned back toward the microphone. She said she could find no misconduct by Devine and then tried to move on to another question. Bill, an old-school journalist, would have none of Alvarez's attempt to change the subject. He blurted out another question, interrupting other people, pressing on Devine's role in the whole scandal. But Alvarez's henchwoman, like a bouncer at a Rush Street bar, approached Bill and told him to stop interrupting.

"If you don't quiet down, you will have to leave," she said.

"She's not answering my question," Bill shot back, even more aggressively, then repeated the question to Alvarez.

I never had more respect for Bill than I did at this moment. Old school, all the way. But Alvarez sidestepped again. She moved on to other questions. No one else in the media would pick up on Bill's question. It was a strange conference, both Alvarez and the media trying to hide their own roles in the scandal. But I still had a card up my sleeve. I was clearly the only police officer in this press conference. This entire Porter episode was not simply the narrative of how a killer was set free and an innocent man imprisoned. Rather, it was the story of how the Chicago Police had been vilified, transformed into monsters in the public imagination. It could not have taken place without the prosecutor's office being co-opted by the wrongful conviction zealots. When these activists got Devine to let Porter out, then arrest Simon, they knew they "owned" the prosecutor's office. In doing so, they could get other killers out, even monsters like

Madison Hobley, which was what they had done. And almost every one of these exonerations was based on some claim of police coercion or misconduct. I knew no one else in the room, including the media, wanted the narrative to go back to the falsely accused police, for in this they were all culpable. So I waited for the right pause to push the questioning exactly into that direction.

"But you have spoken to the prosecutor under Devine who opposed letting Porter out and indicting Simon, haven't you?" I said.

Alvarez paused, started to answer, but then someone else tossed up a question and she went for it. I wondered if some people had been planted to do just that, a common move at Chicago press conferences. I wanted to stand up and confront her, make her answer, the way Bill had just attacked Alvarez's bouncer. I wanted to hit her with the evidence that the media would not bring up, but I didn't know, as a cop, how far I could push it. If I got kicked out of the conference, would Alvarez and her band of attorneys make trouble for me at work? I let it go.

Pussy.

My attention was jerked back to the present when I had to take another steep curve on the California mountain road, coming out of the brush onto a precipice that overlooked miles and miles of mountain that stretched out forever. I paused for a few seconds, my heart racing, then turned the little rental car back toward the mountain, hugging the right wall of the mountain and almost coming to a stop. What if my car caught some gravel and slid over the side? I could imagine the free fall, the crash. So many people in Chicago would be so relieved at my ridiculous death. I could fall so far that no one would ever find the car or my body. No one would ever know what happened to me. One day he was in San Francisco, the next he rented a car and was gone. What theories could emerge about my disappearance and apparent death? Slowly I accelerated again, forcing the car and myself onward, grateful when the road turned downward again, back into the lush overgrowth and away from the cliffs.

How, then, did the release of Simon, something Bill Crawford and I never thought would happen, leave me lost and alone in the mountains of California a few months later? Well, the answer was simple. Overturning the legitimacy of the Anthony Porter exoneration and the conviction of Simon gave me an imaginative freedom, a freedom to tie seemingly disparate events and personalities together. In this newfound freedom, I had come to San Francisco a few days earlier to visit the site of a bombing in 1970, one that left a police sergeant dead and several other police officers badly wounded. In 1970 San Francisco Police Sergeant Brian McDonnell was sitting at a desk at the Park Police Station when someone placed a bomb on the windowsill. The bomb exploded. Most of the wall collapsed next to McDonnell. Shrapnel was sent several blocks away. McDonnell did not die right away. He lingered for several days in the hospital. Investigators believed the bomb was designed to explode after the police were finished with roll call, when the room would have been filled with police officers. But, investigators inferred, the bomb malfunctioned. From early on, a prime suspect in the bombing was Bernardine Dohrn, whose Weather Underground had bombed the Haymarket Memorial in Chicago twice and had set off bombs throughout the country.

Investigators suspected Dohrn because she was believed to be hiding in San Francisco at the time of the bombing. Witnesses described someone leaving the scene who matched her appearance, and the construction of the bomb was similar to other Weather Underground devices. But perhaps the most compelling evidence came from a mole within the Weather Underground group itself. This mole testified that he was told that Dohrn had planted the bomb. FBI agents, now retired, were convinced Dohrn was the offender. The fact that Dohrn had never been brought to justice for the bombing was something that haunted these investigators. Because of it, they had allied with the San Francisco Police Union and requested that federal investigators reopen an investigation into the case in 2006, including advocating that federal prosecutors take another look at the evidence in the case, but the federal prosecutors refused. To this day, the murder of Sergeant McDonnell remains unsolved.

One day about halfway through writing my second book, *Crooked City*, about the Porter case, I was watching a documentary about the Weather Underground. Aware that members of this group had blown up the Haymarket statue in 1969 and then again in 1970, I watched the ample footage of Chicago in the documentary, as many of the group's early exploits took place in the city, and many of their members hailed from Chicago. There was also footage of the aftermath of their bombings throughout the country, in Detroit, New York, whole buildings in rubble, particularly when several members accidentally blew themselves up in a Manhattan townhouse in 1970. It was not unlike the photos I had obtained of the Hobley inferno. The Hobley arson images came back to me, whole sections of the building charred beyond recognition, the bodies of the victims, including two children, charred as they rested on gurneys in the morgue. What, I wondered, must it have been like to go there as a detective and see the victims in both crime scenes. I knew from calls to fire scenes the horrible smell of charred flesh.

Little Philip Hobley was found right next to his mother, Anita. She must have known, within seconds really, that Madison was behind the fire, because he was absent from the apartment as the flames and smoke rushed in. They had been fighting so much, and there had been a fire outside the door a week before. Certainly after that fire, she wondered about her husband. Madison, after all, had threatened arson when Anita took Philip to stay at a friend's house several weeks earlier. All this must have passed through her mind with the smoke billowing in and the heat rising so swiftly, and she realized there was no escape. This time Madison had done it right. And she must have looked over at her son, knowing they would die together. She probably tried to reach for him, or maybe she was just frozen in terror. Maybe even some guilt overwhelmed her, because she failed to acknowledge her misgivings about her husband, failed to see the signs of what was coming.

My thoughts while driving on the isolated California road were interrupted by a faint queasiness, a combination of recalling the Hobley crime scene and the back and forth of the mountain road. I felt I would become nauseous if I remained on this road too much longer. Just as I came to one of these turns, I saw some branches rustling to my right side. As I turned my head toward the sound, I heard the thuds of a large animal moving at what seemed a swift pace. Before I could focus on it, a deer leaped out from the road in full gallop, just inches from the front of my car, which was now stopped. It did not have antlers. Right behind were two little deer, fawns I believe they were called. I could look right into their eyes.

Man, oh, man, I thought. *What if I hit a deer? Where would I push the car to? How would I call for help?*

I looked down at a water bottle on the floor of the passenger side, only one-third full. What was it, thirty more miles back to civilization? Fifty? As the sound of the running deer faded, I took my foot off the brake and began accelerating, my eyes darting back and forth for any more wildlife that might emerge.

My mind returned to the images of the 1970 Manhattan townhouse explosion by the Weather Underground. Investigators discovered a whole cache of dynamite at the scene that miraculously did not explode. If it had, the whole block might have been leveled, killing hundreds. Investigators eventually learned that the group was making the explosives as part of a plan to bomb a military base where a dance was being held. If successful, hundreds of soldiers and their dates or wives could have been killed. Throughout the 1970s, the group bombed dozens of other sites, many of them police stations. They bombed the home of a judge who was presiding over a case involving the Black Panthers, strong revolutionary allies with the Weather Underground. The judge and his family were saved only by the heroic efforts of their neighbors, who got them out of the inferno in time.

At the end of the documentary I had watched about the Weather Underground was a "Where they are now?" section. I sat up from my couch swiftly, one of my cats leaping off my lap, when I learned that Bernardine Dohrn was currently a faculty member at Northwestern University Law School. All this time I had been researching the Porter case and Northwestern's role in it, I had no idea that the university had welcomed a person with Dohrn's background into the school. How had a former accused terrorist bomber ended up working as a professor at one of the country's most prestigious law schools? Because of her criminal past, Dohrn was not allowed to practice law, but here she was, teaching young people. Teaching them exactly what, I wondered. For the next few weeks, I traced the genesis of Dohrn the terrorist into Dohrn the university professor, not unlike the transformation of sociopathic killers into folk heroes, like Anthony Porter, or cops into monsters, like Jon Burge. Talk about revolution. News reports stated that Dohrn was also working on wrongful conviction cases at the school. Wrongful convictions? In all the time I had been reading about the Porter exoneration and the role of David Protess in it, not one media story ever mentioned that an accused terrorist bomber had been hired at the school and was also working on wrongful conviction cases, even when these articles discussed claims of bias and prejudice among cops.

Dohrn's connection to the wrongful conviction movement, I learned, went much deeper. While she was living underground in the '70s, on the run, she and the rest of her group were assisted by the People's Law Office back in Chicago, the same PLO that had been responsible for accusing Jon Burge and his men of being racist torturers. According to several sources, the PLO sent Weather Underground members money and facilitated communication among different cells of the group hiding in various cities. The relationship between the two was actually more intimate, as members of the PLO were close friends with Dohrn and visited her often on the West Coast, including in San Francisco, when she was hiding out there. After the Weather Underground members had bombed several buildings and they knew authorities were looking for them, they considered different ways to disguise themselves while scouting new bombing locations. They hit on the idea of using children as a decoy, believing, rightly, that individuals with children would escape the notice of police officers. The problem was that they didn't have any, so they used the children of a PLO lawyer who was also a close friend.

The PLO's assistance of the Weather Underground, just like their representation of the NATO bombers, painted a different picture of the law firm that was claiming to fight for human rights and justice. Once again, in the hundreds of stories about the PLO making accusations against the police for torture and coercing confessions, one would not find a single story about the law firm's radical past, their ties to the worst domestic terrorists in the nation's history, whose crimes included the possible murder of a police officer. After seeing that Dohrn was an old ally of the PLO and now worked at Northwestern, I couldn't resist. I called Northwestern one morning and left a message for Dohrn. It was one of those shots in the dark, like the time I called the pension board asking if they would put me in touch with the detectives in the Porter case, and they did, and the detectives showed me how their investigation proved Porter was no doubt the killer. While driving down Lake Shore Drive on my way to work a few hours later, Dohrn returned my call. I couldn't believe it. I was a cop, on my way to work, talking to one of the biggest accused domestic terrorists in the country's history. In her radical years, Dohrn was the one who had called for killing "the pigs," to initiate a violent revolution in America, and now she was talking to me on the phone. I could tell she was mostly curious about who I was and what I wanted, so I got to the point quickly. I asked her about her association with members of the PLO, if they had been working with her for a long time. Yes, she said, they had, naming the founding members by their first names, describing how they all went back to the late 1960s and what good friends they were. I asked if she would talk to me again when I was at my desk and I had all my questions before me. She promised she would but never returned another call.

I drove onward, my eyes still darting back and forth across the road, then to the gauges in the car. I fought off the growing conviction that an absurd death on this road, be it attack by a mountain lion, dehydration, or going off the side of the cliff, had a powerful fatefulness about it. This thought increased the sweat on my palms, which I often wiped on my shirt before squeezing the steering wheel again. Despite my anxiety and fear on the mountain road, I confronted this fatefulness, perceiving my own rebellion in doing so. I took stock of what Dohrn, the PLO, and the other wrongful conviction lawyers had done to Chicago, particularly its police officers. At the same time, I took stock of what I had become as a writer. Hadn't Bill Crawford and I—like Protess and the PLO—gotten a convicted killer, Alstory Simon, out of prison? Hadn't we established our own wrongful conviction? And our magic, our wrongful conviction, could withstand the rules of evidence, not hide from them.

This rebellion, in its infancy, was, I believed, a newfound imaginative world. Because of it, I did not spend my vacations on a beach in Mexico. Rather, I traveled to San Francisco on this current trip out west to see the window of the police station where a bomb had been set. I felt as if the burn pattern of the fire so intensely debated in the Hobley case expanded into a larger burn pattern and debate, like the controversy of Dohrn's possible role in the bombing of the 1970 Park Police Station and the gun shots of so many murder cases, like Porter's. In this burgeoning imaginative world, it became crucial for me to see this police station, to ponder the likely route the offender used in his or her arrival and flight. I wanted to talk to any cops who worked at the station to see what they had learned about it, if anyone had ever told them anything about the bombing. Perhaps I would get lucky and there would be some old-timer working in the building who was there for the bombing, perhaps a maintenance guy. In this, I had already hit on some luck. A top union representative had returned my phone calls after I saw his name in some articles about the union demanding that the Feds reopen the criminal investigation against Dohrn. This union official had volunteered to take me to the station and give me a tour, allowing me full access to the building and cops. It meant I could avoid the uncomfortable scenario of suddenly appearing at the station then introducing myself to a busy commander, trying to tell him who I was and what I was about.

But the immersion into the burn patterns was no Sunday jaunt. The more I wandered their trail, the more desolation came alive in me. In wandering into scenes like the Park Station bombing and imagining the destruction there, I was forced to confront my own lostness, one thing that bound me to Dohrn, the Weather Underground, and the People's Law Office. I had read the biographies and memoirs of these radicals, saw that many of them in their youth had wandered about the country, just as I had. If I were honest with myself, I would have to admit that in my own youth, when I was hitchhiking around the country, I agreed with many of the anti-authority tenets of this movement, would maybe even have supported their wrongful conviction claims. It was a horrible truth. I was not like so many other cops who had been raised in a Chicago neighborhood, the son of a cop or a city worker. I had arrived at the job as part of my own wandering, part of my lifelong lostness. In admitting this dark truth that I could have easily ended up sympathizing with one of these groups, I recalled the fact that many Weather Underground members who escaped prison ended up teaching in universities, just like Dohrn. I then recalled how David Protess used his students to get Porter out of prison, to claim Simon was guilty. Many journalists about the city who echoed the wrongful conviction party line graduated from schools where these very activists taught, were likely held spellbound by them. Talk about corruption of the youth. Arriving out west, I could see how easily in my own lost youth people like Dohrn and Protess would have taken hold of my imagination, how I might have joined in on the freeing of a killer. I had gravitated to radical professors in college. I was against everything, shot my mouth off about things I knew absolutely nothing about, and I often took off, hitting the road. It was now painful to recall how fucked up I was, the kind of kid cops I worked with would call a "mope." Thank God I had become a cop.

Returning back over this road the way I had come, the route seemed longer. Had I somehow made a wrong turn? I had now burned up a quarter more tank of gas. Fearing I would run out, I began accelerating slower, coasting downward to save the precious fuel. I could have miles and miles of being lost ahead of me. Perhaps I would be sleeping in the car tonight. The only thing that seemed appropriate for my imagination as I steered the car back and forth on this nameless California road was to continue mentally tracing the path of how I got here. My thoughts had now brought me closer to the present. Just yesterday, I stood outside my hotel in San Francisco waiting for the San Francisco police union official. Kevin pulled up in an SUV, smiled, and said he was going to take me on a trip of the whole city. And he did, first to the police station in the Tenderloin district, then to the Park Station, where they let us right into the back of the station. The officers showed me the wall that had been blown up, where the offender had run off. There was a plaque to Sergeant McDonnell on the building. They gave me a collection of articles from the incident with some background about McDonnell, and they told me that some of his family members had toured the station a few years earlier. They gave me the names of these relatives and told me they lived in Seattle, where I was heading two days later. Kevin didn't just give me a tour of the police stations. He took me through Haight-Ashbury, showed me where Jimi Hendrix lived, where the Grateful Dead hung out. He knew all the hippie store owners, gave them big hugs when he came in. As we drove into different neighborhoods, he recalled police officers who had been shot there, telling me the story of the shooting in detail, because, as a union rep, he had responded to it.

After Kevin dropped me off at the hotel, there was one more visit I had to make before leaving the city. I cleaned up, then took a cab to the City Lights Bookstore, the famous center of the beatnik literary movement. It was packed with customers, young and old. The walls were filled with pictures of Allen Ginsberg, Jack Kerouac, Lawrence Ferlinghetti— writers I had tried desperately to embrace when I was young.

I had heard that Bernardine Dohrn had hung out at the bookstore when she was on the run. These writers were once outcasts, barely able to get published. Now their bookstore was flooded with people, the cash registers humming. I walked around the store, looking at the books, the photos of the beatniks from years gone by. How strange to walk through this bookstore as a cop/writer. My dislike for this movement moved to the forefront. I hated, for example, the beatnik faith in inspiration over craft, spontaneity over discipline, the fact that Kerouac claimed he wrote his novel on a long paper roll typed in a frenzy of one long draft, as if good writing, or any art, could realize itself in one draft. But what troubled me most about his most famous work, *On the Road*, was the hero Neal Cassady. Described as a kind of prophet by Kerouac as he and Cassady wandered about the country, I eventually saw as I became a cop the familiar paradigm of a criminal mind in Cassady's drug binging, unemployment, refusal to own up to his responsibilities, and the cruelty with which he treated people, particularly women, and felt no remorse. *On the Road* had been an inspiration to youths. I thought about the students in Protess's class at Northwestern, spellbound by him, students gravitating to Dohrn as if she were some kind of hero.

So I grabbed a few postcards, paid for them, and walked out in front of the store, where I took a selfie. The visit to the City Lights Bookstore was a mistake. This beatnik bookstore brought up once again the lostness of my own life. I had failed to get my second book accepted by a publisher, selling the copies out of the trunk of my car. The sun was going down over the bay. It was such a beautiful, easygoing city, yet

I wanted to be far away from it. Once I had dreamed of regularly publishing with the University of Chicago Press, never having to worry about being accepted by publishers, agents, or editors again. Now I was a literary fugitive. I waved down a cab and headed back to the hotel. It was an old hotel, where I could open the window. So I did, lying on my bed before the sun even went down, until I drifted into a light sleep with lots of dreams I could not afterward recall.

My mood was no better the next morning, I now recalled as I wheeled the car through yet another S-curve, even though the sun came out as I pulled onto Interstate 5, just beginning the trip that now had me steeped in recollections that were rapidly catching up to the present time. Sipping my coffee as I set out, I figured a touristy ride on a country road would set me right, the lovely sights from my little four-cylinder rental car with a full tank of gas. So I pulled over, spotted a blue road on the map a few miles ahead, cutting all the way from the interstate to the coast. The thick blue line on the map looked like a vibrant vein in a healthy person. So I turned off onto it, heading west once again. It was a beautiful road, one winery after another, acres and acres of vineyards. It was too early for any of them to be open, but I promised myself I would stop at one in Oregon or Seattle and stock up. Though eager to get to the coast, I was also excited about mountains I would pass through before getting there. It had been so long since I had seen any mountains. But I could not relish them as I might because the roads in California echoed the feeling of lostness that began at the Park Street Station and then shadowed me again at the City Lights Bookstore. In my youth I had hitchhiked around this part of the country, filled with the mythology and false promise of fulfillment of the beatnik writers. Here I was again, in my rental car, fighting back the growing shame and regret of my previous selves.

Past the wineries, the road became less congested. The hills grew larger. The road began to wind a little bit, requiring me to pay close attention. This would not be a relaxed trip. I found myself gripping the wheel harder than usual. I turned the radio down and cracked the window a little more. After a half hour or so, the first signs I had seen in many miles indicated I was entering a state park. Upward I climbed, the hills now mountains, shifting my little rental car into a lower gear before I emerged out on a bridge high up in the air, where I could see towering mountains for miles. *Man, these are big fucking mountains*, I thought. I passed over a river or a reservoir of some kind. Along this reservoir below me I saw some RVs, the only vehicles I had spotted in a long time. Being so high up and looking downward, I got a little dizzy. After the state park, I moved right into the heart of the mountains, with such tight turns I was leaning in the car right and left to negotiate them, almost coming to a complete stop on some of them to make the turn. I would be facing down an immense slope one minute, then upward another. Within a few miles, there were no longer guardrails along the side of the road. I could catch glimpses of huge cliffs just off the road. One slip-up, one turn with too much gravel could send me over the edge.

That wasn't the only thing. Particularly on the turns, I could not determine if there was enough room for a car coming the other way, especially a truck. So with each turn, I feared the grille of a large truck pushing my sorry four-cylinder rental over the side. There was nowhere to pull over, not even enough room to turn around, so I just kept going. If this wasn't a living metaphor of my life, if this road didn't give form to my inner turmoil, I didn't know what would. Shifting the gears constantly because of the immense slopes, I stole quick looks to the temperature gauge, then to the fuel gauge, reassuring myself over and over that the engine was performing well and I would not run out of gas. Another quick glance at my cell phone sent my heart racing even more. There was no signal. I could not call for help. What if I broke down or got in an accident, striking a deer or something? I started thinking in headlines, never a good sign.

"Off-Duty Chicago Cop Mauled by Bears." "Stranded Tourist Dies of Snake Bite." "Falling Rocks Kill Chicago Man" . . . *rental car not powerful enough for mountain range, authorities say.*

On the map it looked like a short drive from the interstate to the coast, but now I realized the winding roads meant I was making little progress at all. This could take hours. What if it got dark? What if there was a storm? What if fog rolled in? How could my car handle a flash flood? Just then a truck came from the other direction. I put my car as close to the edge of the mountain as possible. The four-wheeler passed within inches. There were two people in the truck, a couple, gawking down at me dumbfounded, their expression asking a rhetorical question: "What the fuck is that idiot doing driving alone on this road in such a little car?" Then it was gone. Only pride kept me from hitting the horn, getting them to stop, and begging for their help. Larger and larger the mountains became. *How fucking big are these mountains,* I asked myself. Trees and bushes grew out, slapping against the car. Any minute a moose or a deer, perhaps even a bear, would run out in front of me or would be sitting on the road around a corner. What about mountain lions, I wondered. Were there mountain lions out here? *Of course there are, you dumb fuck. You are in the mountains. That's where mountain lions live.* Were there also cougars, or were cougars and mountain lions the same thing? I couldn't remember. Were they watching me taking the corners at five miles an hour, waiting for the inevitable screw-up on my part that would leave me stranded?

To my great relief, I spotted a few driveways with mailboxes on them as I turned a few corners. *Now I must be getting close to civilization again,* I thought. *Perhaps the coast is just up the road a piece.* But turning another corner, I was shocked to see a gate across the road and a dirt path beyond it. An old sign, barely hanging on the gate, said: "Road Ends."

"No shit," I said out loud, slapping the steering wheel. "Perhaps you could have told me that sixty miles ago."

I stared at it, absolutely unsure of what to do. Did I have to go all the way back to the interstate and start over? Maybe, I thought in my panicked state, this two-wheel path was the way to go. As soon as I thought about it, I castigated myself. *Sure, a dirt road will take you through the mountains to the ocean, you dumbshit. You'll be dead in an hour.* I backed the car up, turned it around by going back and forth many times, and drove back the route I had taken, aware from experience how treacherous, how dangerous it was to be so lost.

And so in my thoughts I lurched back into the present, retracing a road whose name I did not know in the mountain ranges of northern California, now having to take a piss so badly, I feared I would do it in my pants. Just then, I spotted a two-lane path and pulled onto it. If there was a home around, I couldn't see it. I left the car running because I had a paranoid sense that it might not start again, and even so, I also rolled the window all the way down.

Don't lock yourself out of your car now, dumbass.

Outside the car, but not too far outside in case I needed it for refuge from a charging bear or mountain lion, I whipped Little Joe out and took the longest piss, one of those two-large-coffee pisses, careful not to get caught up in any shifting mountain winds. Regardless, one large swirling breeze caught me anyway and sent some of the spray back at me. I tried to turn away but only moved the flap of my jeans over Little Joe, pissing on myself worse than what the wind did. I turned back toward my car as I was putting him back in my pants, then leaned against the car, my panic increasing as I thought about driving back on this road. Perhaps it was better just to remain here and wait for a car, if one ever showed up. I would have to wave down the car. Since the road curved so much, they would only have a moment to register me. They would not be able to see my car parked on the path, that I was a motorist. Because of this, I risked looking like someone who simply appeared out of the woods, some crazed man. Just then I remembered I'd spilled raspberry on my shirt from a Danish I'd eaten while driving earlier that morning when I pulled out of San Francisco. I looked down at my shirt. The raspberry stain was still red, like blood. I looked down farther and noticed my now wet fly was still open. A hand went up to my chin and cheeks. I had not shaved for four days. I looked like a cult murderer, like a Manson follower, fresh from a kill, some crazy fucking revolutionary emerging from the woods. I imagined trying to wave down a driver on this lonely, dangerous road. I would have to explain myself in a few moments, an impossible task.

"Can you help me? I'm a cop. I'm lost. There was a bombing in 1970. A sergeant died. It's tied to Chicago, you see. It's all tied to Chicago. I'm from Chicago. There is a revolution. That's not blood. It's raspberry. A Danish, I had a Danish. It was delicious. The food out here is really good. I peed on myself. It was an accident. Two cups of coffee, you see. You know how it is. I can explain everything. It's actually quite funny if you think about it."

The door locks of any motorist would click, then they would speed off. They might even report me to the police. A helicopter might start looking for me. The dogs would come. I would be on the run.

I zipped up my pants, then my jacket, covering up the raspberry stain.

Part of my panic was rooted in the fact that this unfolding catastrophe brought back such memories, as if this was always the essential condition of my life. Imaginative freedom, my ass. I was trapped in my own fate, just like everyone else. This whole excursion was doomed from the outset. *But then, no*, I thought. *Don't give in. This is only a habit of mind.* I remained against the car, trying to calm down, and reminded myself again why I had come to San Francisco.

What must it have been like for Bernardine Dohrn the days after the bombing at Park Station, if she did indeed do it? How had she talked herself into believing it was a good thing to have murdered McDonnell, who suffered terribly in the hospital before he died? Just a few months earlier, her comrades had blown up the Haymarket Memorial. And what must it have been like for Protess when he set Porter free? What would he say if Porter killed again? What if Porter murdered a child? And how anxious it must have been for Protess to know that someday someone would unravel the evidence of what had truly taken place. And now that had happened. And what about the freeing of Hobley? What it must be like to have that hanging over your head. I looked up and around. How far was the coast? How far did I have to go on this road? Perhaps I should just go back to San Francisco and fly home, even if it cost thousands. I paused and considered things.

Life on the road is stark. In the solitude of standing next to an on-ramp, for hours, or walking down some road with no particular destination, no real pursuit or ambition, one lives in a vivid immediacy, like the Pacific Ocean over one's shoulder or a rainstorm observed from under a bridge in Idaho. The truth is that I loved the road, loved this vivid immediacy. But there is always one nagging question for every wandering soul: Is one moving toward something or running from it? The question goes to one's intentions, for it asks if one is encountering life on the road with an open heart or is one little more than a refugee or a fugitive.

Leaning on my rental car, I admitted to myself I was still on the road. I had never left it. I had lived much of my life as a refugee, in flight from the demons that haunted me. Being lost on this road in California brought it all back. But I was still on the road. Only now I grabbed some keys to a squad car and wandered a neighborhood every afternoon, letting crime and the law guide me. I didn't want to be a cop; I needed to be one. I needed to wander the world with some logic, not on some dizzy fugitive flight on the West Coast. Patrol was often a dismal, brutal trip, but it held out the hope of something authentic. How ironic that, in becoming a cop, I had become the revolutionary. I lived a covert life, as subversive as anyone who ever hung out at City Lights, including Dohrn.

So I stood up, looked around. *Buck up, you fucking pussy*, I told myself. *You're a fucking cop. You are not broke anymore, living on the road in California as you once were. You are not under the spell of bullshit books and second-rate teachers. You have a credit card and a condo, a laptop with a manuscript on it.* And just then, I could hear a car coming, and I raised my hand for them to stop, which they did. I would, in fact, have to retrace my path, they said, all the way the back to the state park. There, right past the bridge, they told me, was another road that would go to the coast. And so I went back, found that other road, and headed west again. This road was actually worse than the one I had just been on, steeper, with more turns, more dangerous curves, but I kept my eyes on the road and on the gauges in the car, shifted carefully, and made my way. I wouldn't give up. It took several hours before I started to see little homes and trailers. My hands were sore from gripping the wheel. I was exhausted when I rounded one corner and there was the Pacific Ocean in front of me, blue and vast, the sun fading into the water line. I went north just a few miles until I saw a turnoff where you could watch the sea lions sunning on the rocks, floating on their backs, and casually diving for fish.

I made it.

Chapter 12

INTERLUDE

Sirens approached. There were more voices murmuring above me, a crowd gathering. I could hear some of them clearly.

"It's disgusting, like he was burned or something."

"The smell is awful."

"His fly is open."

The detectives would eventually come, as would the evidence technicians, especially if they learned that I had been a cop. So would the media. Oh Christ, the media. They would flood the place, barely able to hide their joy at my death. Secretly they were hoping I did burn to death. They wished it was a slow burning.

"Cop with Anger Issues over Police Corruption Found Dead."

I shifted my gaze to the east, out toward the lake, without moving my body or eyes. You can do those things when you are dead. In fact, the power to see things beyond physical limitations increases the longer you are dead, the more you decay. Every few minutes I sensed the increase of this power. Because of this, I wondered if the difference between life and death was a question of degree. One was very much alive or very much dead, or somewhere in between. This made sense, because I believed that the dead had spoken to me from the other side when I was living, the dead ones who had been murdered and watched their killers walk free. They were stopped in their journey to where the fully dead go, waiting until things got cleared up before they could move on. But they never got cleared up. Chicago held them in this interminable way station, the city's menacing way of showing the power of its corruption midway between both worlds. But since the recently dead ones were not so far gone, they could still be heard. They could still speak in the city. They weren't like the long dead and buried, who had to convince a worm or bug about the secret of their death, hoping somehow, someday the bug would surface and get the word out to the living. But this rarely happened, because no one listens to a bug or a worm.

Now it looked as if I were joining these suspended dead. The city pulled me back with its covert power over the currents of Lake Michigan, making me float onto the rocks where all the students could see me in this state.

Motherfucker, I thought.

This suspension between the living world and the dead one sent me into a panic and rage. I could not exist this way. If the students above me got off the sidewalk, walked down, and looked closely at me, they would see I was perspiring, that my eyes were darting back and forth. I had to get out of the city, out of this suspension that I knew was planned for me. The city torments people like me by making them remain this way, unable to move in a grave while the city's corruption goes on all about them like a kind of dance, the fact that they know what is truly happening tormenting them in their silence. The city laughs at them, taunts them, the way wrongful conviction lawyers taunt the families of murder victims, by getting the cases reconsidered again and again, though each legal proceeding determines the original offender was guilty, just like in the Porter and Hobley cases. This dance also moves the tormented dead into a madness that not even death will end, because they are already deceased.

So I determined I had to escape with whatever life force still remained in me. Just as I made this decision, I perceived some water hitting my left shoulder. I turned my gaze to Lake Michigan. The water was rough and rising, working its way toward me. Waves were hitting the rocks. It seemed as if some force were reaching out to help me. At that moment the world had boiled down to a duality, religious in nature, as if this force were God trying to rescue me from the evil I was now heading into. This was ironic in one of those otherworldly ways, for I had always been a pretentious atheist in my younger years, but, after investigating the wrongful conviction cases, I had come to question this atheism. There must be some judgment, I figured. There must also be some forgiveness and redemption. There must be. I found that the older I got, the more I wanted to be forgiven. So you think I was gonna let this opportunity go by, this chance to get the hell out of

Chicago? No way. I wasn't that stupid. I could hear the voices of coworkers approaching and the sound of their radios, could hear the diesel engines of the fire department. The water was coming closer and there was a wind off the lake.

Okay, I thought. *Wait for the right wave, then turn with all your energy into it.*

And that's exactly what I did, with great timing. The wave embraced me and lifted me off the rocks. As it did so, people above began to gasp and shout, yelling at the firemen and cops to hurry up.

Fuck you, I thought about saying, but rejected the idea because it seemed as if the hand of God was helping me out, and such taunting might make him change his mind. It was time I learned about being pious, another shortcoming of my living existence. The problem was that as the water receded, it set me down on another rock, a rock farther from the shoreline but nevertheless leaving me still rescuable by the cops and firemen. Already I could hear them plotting different ways of getting to me and bringing me up, as if they were doing me a favor by rescuing me. *Rescuing me?* I wanted to shout at them. *Rescuing? Let me get the fucking living hell out of here.*

Don't stop now, I said to the waves, and they didn't let me down. An even bigger one came, splashed over me, and pulled me into the water, the screams of the students and now also professors still ringing in my ears. Their voices were now barely audible in the water, a silence emerging that I loved. All I had to do now was catch some current to take me away from this area, for I knew the marine unit was already looking for me, and if they caught me, I might be stuck in the city for an eternity.

If I could escape, I would be on the road again. I could end up in Indiana or Michigan, washed up on some beach, being eaten by birds. That was fine with me because then I could go where the dead go, still on the road, still figuring things out. I could perhaps understand more clearly the author of this current that was rescuing me. There were only a few hours of sunlight left. If I could be pushed in this current far enough away from shore, I might remain undiscovered until darkness. Then the marine unit would have even more trouble finding my body. They would need lights. The notion of escape was thrilling. As it came over me, I felt the undertow even stronger. I felt it keep my body close to the sandy bottom of the lake as I moved into deeper water. I even saw the bottom of the marine unit boat as it tossed its anchor in preparation of a search for me. I couldn't help but smile at the irony. Here I was, escaping the police, myself a fugitive.

The scenery improved. Close to shore there was a lot of debris in the water, floating on the top and at the bottom, trash from picnics on the beach, paper residue from exploded fireworks. Farther out, it was just rocks, curious fish, some of whom were smiling at me as if they were glad to see me. I had no idea that the largely dead could feel such joy as I did in the gentle waves moving across the lake, a few miles offshore. But just as this joy emerged, I felt the current subside. I became aware that the small waves around me were likely pushing me back to the city, ever so slowly, and that my hopes of an exit from the city were doomed. As the waves slowly moved me back toward the shore, memories rose up, not in any specific narrative form, but as pure images, separately or in a collage, intense. Sometimes they were clear, other times vague, barely decipherable. And there were voices with them. Oh, such voices. All of them washed over me like the water around me. I found myself weeping in the water, shocked that the dead could ache so.

Chapter 13

SUBPOENAS

The county jail and courthouses at Twenty-Sixth and California are bleak, a vast complex of courts and prosecutors' offices surrounded by prison units of various security levels, all connected by underground tunnels that allow county sheriffs to shuttle the thousands of inmates to their hearings every day. The buildings teem with gang members, families of victims and the accused, lawyers, cops, detectives, sheriffs who keep order, and often an army of media on the ground floor awaiting a decision in a high-profile criminal case. I had been coming to this courthouse on and off for more than a decade, more so when I first was on the job and made more arrests. Now, since I work foot patrol far up north, I hardly ever come here. When cops come to these courthouses, they mostly park in a garage or a lot next to it, walk with a jersey or shirt over their uniform, and avoid eye contact with anyone who is not a cop. In particular, they avoid eye contact or conversation with anyone on the crowded elevators. For a cop, there is a kind of dread in entering the building, the realization that the worst thing that could ever happen for any police officer would be arriving in this building as a defendant. This is a felony court building. Any cop charged in this court is likely looking at prison time. The media gather on the first floor where the accused must walk past them on the way in or out of the building, dozens of cameras locked on them and reporters shouting questions, trying to block their path.

It was with a particular, overwhelming dread, therefore, that I walked up the steps of the courthouse and entered the building with my cousin serving as my lawyer, called here not because of any police work, but because of my writing. I was here because G. Flint Taylor, the lead attorney at the People's Law Office, had subpoenaed all my correspondence with Jon Burge in the course of my research for this book about the Hobley arson. I was heading into a courtroom to fight the subpoena, the notion of handing over my private correspondence with Burge to Taylor infuriating. How did it come to this, I wondered. In writing about these cases, I was a journalist myself. I had a few articles published about them. How could the courts allow a lawyer to get the records of a writer researching his book? Taylor's claim for getting them was that he was searching for evidence that might shed light on the latest round of wrongful conviction claims against Burge he was arguing in court.

How ludicrous. Even if Burge were the racist monster Taylor said he was, would Burge send me a message on my computer saying, "Yeah, Marty, we tortured all these guys, but that's just between you and me. Okay, buddy? That will be our little secret." And if he had sent me a message like that, would I still be writing about him in my book and on my blog? Would I risk my reputation as a cop and a writer to lie so much about a monster, a man I had met in person only once? No incriminating exchange ever occurred between us. Rather, we spoke on the phone, Burge in Florida, fresh out of prison, and me in Chicago, going over Taylor's trajectory from working with the likes of the Weather Underground and the Black Panthers to wrongful conviction attorney. We were establishing the means by which Taylor had used Burge to manufacture his wrongful conviction mythology. Later that day in court, Taylor would tell the judge he wanted to look at the correspondence for some sign of "racial animus," as if Burge, even if he were some racist, would show his hand to me. Burge had never made a racist statement to me in writing or on the phone, ever.

I figured there were several reasons why Taylor wanted to look at my correspondence with Burge. One was that he was simply putting pressure on me, knowing I would have to hire an attorney and go to court. Another was more complicated. Burge and his men had long since refused to testify in any of Taylor's wrongful conviction bids, repeatedly taking the Fifth on the advice of their lawyers. Getting Burge and his men to remain silent was one of the great accomplishments of the wrongful conviction movement, for it meant that Taylor and his supporters could make claims against the police without having to worry about the police contradicting them. It had not always been so. The detectives in the Porter case demanded that the city not settle with Porter's attorneys. They fought to retry the case in civil court and won, the jury seeing clearly that Porter committed the murders. So it was with the Hobley case. The entire argument that Hobley was innocent was based on the claim that detectives had abused Hobley. But the detectives fought for the city to contest Hobley's civil lawsuit in a trial, just as the detectives in the Porter case had done. It was a powerful sign that the detectives had not abused Hobley. If they had, a civil trial would have risked revealing evidence of this abuse, evidence that could ultimately become criminal charges against them. The last thing a guilty cop wanted was for a civil trial to go forward. They would want a settlement in which they admitted no guilt.

But the Hobley detectives were foiled in their quest to go to trial. Right before it was to begin, city attorneys announced that they had engaged in secret negotiations with Hobley's attorneys and had reached a settlement. The detectives were furious. They believed they had been betrayed by the city. Here was a chance to clear their names and, most of all, to reveal the corruption at the heart of the wrongful conviction movement, to show the public unequivocally that a mass murderer had been set free on fraudulent claims. Betrayals like this by the city against the police, along with the power that Taylor and his cronies had over the courts and political system, eventually left detectives concluding that their only option was to take the Fifth, lest they end up in prison, like Burge. With the detectives silent, the public relations campaign against the police was wide open, and Taylor took full advantage of it. He could say anything, and did. He preached about Burge and his men being racist torturers to anyone who would listen, including students. He claimed that these men continued torturing suspects even after allegations against them were made public, as if they were so sadistic that they could not refrain from abusing African American men even when they were being investigated for it. I believed Taylor's bid to obtain Burge's correspondence with me was an attempt to get statements that Taylor might be able to present as something culpable against Burge, and Burge would not reply to them because he was still pleading the Fifth.

Taylor, I felt, was also trying to vilify me. A few months earlier he and the PLO had scored one of their greatest victories in the city. They had compelled the City Council to approve reparations to so-called victims of Burge torture. It meant that even offenders who could not sue the city because the statute of limitations had expired got another bite at the apple. Convicted killers as far back as the 1970s could claim that Burge and his men had abused them and be awarded reparations money. One of the so-called victims of torture was Darrell Cannon. A career criminal, Cannon was sentenced to a hundred years for the 1978 murder of a man who owned a toy store. Despite his hundred-year sentence, Cannon was released in just over a decade, then he killed again. Burge's men conducted the investigation for that second murder as an adult. Now Cannon was getting a payout from the city, three decades after the crime. Cops were furious at the vote by the City Council. In my conversations with Burge, I suggested he publish a statement on my blog about the reparations, and he agreed, so long as his attorney approved. The three of us went back and forth on email before we decided on a statement. This was the first time Burge broke his silence about the allegations against him.

This is what Burge wrote for the blog:

REPARATIONS?

What about reparations for the families of the African American victims of the heinous crimes perpetrated by the scum who now demand reparations? This entire scenario is being manipulated by lawyers like G. Flint Taylor and his ilk. They have been getting rich for years filing specious lawsuits against Chicago Police Officers, the City of Chicago and other government entities. They know that 99% of the time the City will settle the lawsuit rather than go to trial because it's cheaper. The City never admits wrongdoing on their part or the part of the individual defendants (police officers) when they settle.

Evidence is slowly emerging that clearly shows what happened to the dedicated Chicago Police Detectives who fought, as best we could, the worst, most violent predators on the South Side of Chicago. To understand, all one has to do is review the long record of unethical criminal activity exhibited by academics and students at Northwestern University, particularly in the case of Anthony Porter, a man obviously guilty of two murders, but released from custody after an "investigation" conducted by NU professor David Protess and his students. There has never been a case with more blatant Subornation of Perjury than when they framed an innocent man, Alstory Simon, for the crime committed by Porter.

State's Attorney Alvarez admitted the criminal behavior on the part of the crew from Northwestern when she announced she was dropping the case against Alstory Simon and petitioning for his release. This is not an unusual instance on the part of the Northwestern crew, and slowly emerging evidence will condemn their participation in helping free other guilty criminals.

Working to free guilty, vicious criminals by the likes of G. Flint Taylor and others like him, as well as the Northwestern cabal, all with a radical political agenda, has created a thriving cottage industry in Chicago. These private attorneys grow rich because the City of Chicago is afraid to defend the lawsuits filed by these human vultures. Ask the mayor and City Council members how many relatives of the victims of these crimes they spoke with before deciding on their "Reparations."

The chief spokesmen for G. Flint Taylor's reparations campaign are Darrell Cannon and Anthony Holmes. Cannon is a former El Rukn General who has been convicted of three separate murders in his long career, pleading guilty to the last one after cutting a deal for "time served." His first murder conviction was as a juvenile, so the police can't mention it, but I can. He still stands convicted of all three murders.

Anthony Holmes also had a long career. During one of his first visits to prison he was the "Barn Boss" at

Statesville, when Statesville was the toughest prison in Illinois. That means he ran the prison. He was on Chicago's "10 Most Wanted" list when he was arrested for Murder. He subsequently gave a court reported confession to the crime. There was NO MOTION TO SUPPRESS the confession. In fact there was no mention in public by Holmes that he was "tortured" until over a decade later, after he met G. Flint Taylor. By the way, he claims he did 30 years for the murder. The truth is he was paroled after 11 years and got busted making a hand-to-hand dope buy from an undercover agent shortly after he was released. He went back to the joint for the Parole Violation and served a few more years. Holmes was one of the leaders of a group called "The Royal Family," which consisted of 31 ex-cons who patterned their operations after the mafia. They committed a string of commercial armed robberies unheard of at the time, and, if one of their crew got caught, they simply murdered the witnesses. I find it hard to believe that the City's political leadership could even contemplate giving "Reparations" to human vermin like them.

The media's long silence on these activities makes them complicit in the fraud being perpetrated on Chicago and the citizenry. When the true evidence finally rules the day and the record is set straight, the people who conspired to free a man like Madison Hobley, who was awarded seven million dollars by the City after he burned seven people to death,

including his wife and infant son, will have to pay
the piper.
At that time I believe I and all the outstanding men
and women I had the privilege of working with, as
well as the Chicago Police Department itself, will be
vindicated.

Someone in the media eventually called Burge and got
him to admit he made the statement. It flew around the city.
The next day, all the papers covered it. They immediately ran
to Taylor for a quote. Taylor assailed Burge's statement,
repeating his claims of torture and abuse in the *Chicago
Sun-Times*:

Taylor denounced Burge as a "convicted perjurer and
liar." He noted that, just a month ago, Burge took the
Fifth Amendment once again rather than "tell these
lies and commit this perjury under oath and run the
risk of going back to jail where he truly belongs to
spend the rest of his life. . . ."
"He is clearly a serial human rights violator who has
committed racist crimes against humanity too
numerous to count. And this attack on the men who
have so bravely stood up to him — and who a jury
and a federal judge relied upon to send him to the
penitentiary — only underscores how disgraceful and
cowardly his unsworn statements . . . slandering me,
my fellow lawyers and these clients are," Taylor said.
"I stand ready to go anywhere, any time, any place to
place him under oath and to ask him point-blank

whether he tortured Anthony Holmes and whether
he was responsible for the torture of Darrell Cannon
and 115-to-120 other African-American men who have
documented proof that he and his co-conspirators
tortured them."

Taylor was outraged by the suggestion that he and his
fellow attorneys representing torture victims are
money-grubbers.

"We have been committed to this for over 2½ decades
— not to make money, but because we are firmly
committed to exposing racist crimes against humanity. And the people who have joined with us include
Amnesty International and a wide range of other
organizations who . . . see his crimes for what they
are," Taylor said.

"He says the truth will come out. The truth has come
out. That's why the city has acted as it has. No matter
what kind of cowardly statements Burge may make
under cover of darkness, it is not going to change the
public record of his and his fellow officers' crimes."

None of the media paused and asked in their articles on
Burge's statement about the fact that Cannon had murdered
three people, that he never claimed he was tortured at the
time of his arrest. He only mentioned torture years afterward
when he met G. Flint Taylor. None of them responded to
Burge's statements about the Hobley arson.

In my view, there was yet another, far more ominous
reason Taylor was trying to get into my emails. Once the
Porter case fell apart, a host of others also looked suspect,

including four other exonerations that Governor George Ryan granted in 2003, four years after Porter was released. In letting the four inmates go, Ryan made an impassioned speech, citing the Porter exoneration as a primary influence in his decision. One of those four men he released was Madison Hobley. But in 2014, eleven years after Ryan released Hobley and three other prisoners, the Porter case unraveled. The prosecutor had rejected the tactics used by Northwestern's Innocence Project in getting Alstory Simon to confess and threw out Simon's conviction. It became impossible to ignore the corruption in these other exonerations, including Hobley's.

This was a threat to Taylor and his entire movement, for Hobley was not just an outrage in that he got away with mass murder. It was also the case that got Taylor and his wrongful conviction comrades the golden calf: the criminal conviction of Jon Burge.

Here is how it happened. In the course of Hobley's civil lawsuit against the city, where Hobley was claiming he'd been abused despite there being no evidence to support his claim, Burge denied ever abusing any suspects in his career. Burge had been sued twice civilly for abusing the cop killer Andrew Wilson, but was not found guilty in either trial. For decades afterward, Taylor and his cohorts had been desperately seeking ways to get Burge indicted. Finally, the Hobley case offered that opportunity. Federal prosecutors bowed to the pressure of the wrongful conviction movement, just as the city had in the Porter case, and indicted Burge for perjury in his denial of torturing anyone, despite his never having been convicted of any abuse. Burge and the police from that era were shocked, especially since all these cops believed that Hobley was guilty of setting the fire and had proven it in court. Could it be, they wondered, that the Feds would use the case of a man who incinerated his own family as a tactic to finally indict Burge? Incredibly, they did. But now, with the Porter case imploding, a clear pattern was emerging of corruption at Northwestern University in their drive to frame the police and undermine the justice system. What would happen to Taylor and the entire wrongful conviction movement if the misconduct in the Porter case led to the reexamination of the Hobley case? What would it mean if the Hobley exoneration was also revealed as a fraud? It would mean that the entire criminal conviction of Burge was based upon a lie. We had already initiated a trail of evidence from the Porter case that could lead to Hobley's. Such an outcome would be the implosion of Taylor's world, the entire mythology upon which his revolution had been built—all the way back to the 1960s—called into question. This was, in my mind, the key reason Taylor was coming after me. I believed he was trying to discredit me for supporting Burge, and he was looking for something in the correspondence between us that would allow him to do so.

With such "evidence," he could mount a campaign to discredit my claims about the Hobley case. I could see him greedily clicking through my computer, eyeing anything in there that he could twist against me. What an invasion of my privacy. Now I was in a courtroom, about to go before a judge where that very possibility could become real. As my cousin and I entered the courtroom, there was Taylor with one of his partners, Joey Mogul. They were whispering to one another.

Taylor and his minions had so much influence over the courts and politicians. Prosecutors, judges, aldermen, and city attorneys were all terrified of them. They could get killers out of prison, as well as convincing governors to release multiple offenders from prison, and leverage reparations from the city. Perhaps, I thought, this was it. Maybe my campaign to reveal the fraudulence in the movement was coming to an end. Maybe getting Alstory Simon out of prison was the only thing we would accomplish. Perhaps everything would remain status quo in the city for decades, and then forty years from now, some bright student or academic would pore through the record and see the injustice that had been committed, just as Timothy Messer-Kruse had pored through the record of the Haymarket bombing more than a century afterward and discovered that the police and prosecutors had gotten the case right all along, that they had fairly investigated and convicted many of the perpetrators.

In this diminished frame of mind, I looked over at my cousin. The last thing I wanted to do was bring my family into this battle, for my cousin was older than I and had been close to my father in a manner I never was. My cousin had been an extremely successful attorney, carving out a law practice on his own. I, on the other hand, had been an enduring disappointment. I had had to make the desperate phone call to my cousin a few days earlier asking for representation, as my first lawyer and I had parted ways because I wanted to appeal the judge's decision, but the attorney took a new job and could no longer represent me for free. In the courtroom, I could feel my father's eyes on me.

The courtroom was filled with felons, attorneys, sheriffs,

and other cops I did not know. My cousin knew little of the
thirty-year story behind these cases. As I sat in one of the
front rows of wooden benches, I wondered about the shoe
being on the other foot, if a lawyer representing a cop or the
city tried to get emails from a journalist or writer. The
community of journalists and writers in the city would go
apeshit. There would be columns in the papers about the
importance of the free press, the right to privacy. There
would likely be protests. In fact, it had already happened. In
2010 Cook County Prosecutor Anita Alvarez had subpoenaed
Protess and his students' records after she became suspicious
about his claims in another wrongful conviction case. Protess
and Northwestern claimed they were protected because
Protess and his students were working as journalists. An
avalanche of condemnation followed in the wake of this
subpoena, the chorus of academics, activists, and public
figures assailed Alvarez. But the judge ruled in her favor,
saying Protess and his students were not working as journalists. They were working as investigators for the defendant,
she ruled. It was these subpoenas that eventually led to Protess's downfall, as they revealed evidence that he had lied
about his investigation, even altered evidence. But there was
no such outcry for a patrolman working as a writer. On the
contrary, it was a mark of how low I had sunk in the city as a
writer that this hearing was even taking place.

All this was weighing down on me in the courtroom as I
stood up and walked in front of the judge's bench with my
cousin: the demise of my writing career, it leading me to the
city's criminal courts; the feeling that my father was in the
courtroom, disgusted with me; the lives of my friends who

had been destroyed by Taylor and his comrades. But at the same time I knew that Porter was guilty of the murders and Alstory Simon was not. I had seen the crime scene photos of the Porter murders, of the Hobley arson. I knew that we had gotten Simon out of prison and that Madison Hobley committed the arson in 1987. My depression turned swiftly into rage. Did these people truly care whether someone was rightly or wrongfully convicted? Taylor and his associate Mogul were approaching the bench as well, walking close by. I glared at Taylor, my anger peaking. This was the guy whose law firm represented the NATO bombers, a lawyer who had ruined the lives of hundreds of cops, cops I had interviewed in dozens of diners and bars, convinced they had never abused anyone. Now this clown was coming after me, trying to destroy my writing life. When Taylor walked by, he brushed up against me. I leaned into him, just a touch with my shoulder, and gave the slightest shove, so that he had to move from one foot to another. My rage welled up like—I couldn't deny it—like a fire.

It was right then, standing before the judge, that I became aware of just how badly I needed the law, a real, living law, not this dog-and-pony show at Twenty-Sixth and California. Not only would such a law preserve me from the inhumanity of my fantasies that arose in the courtroom, but it would also force an honesty upon me, the truth that I could have gone down the same road as the young people who followed Taylor and the wrongful conviction overlords with such admiration. I could look back at the stages of my confused life, all my furtive movements about the country, and see how I could have been taken in by the mythology of this movement. How attractive it would have been to be a hero who garnered the release of an innocent man. Perhaps I could have become a figure like Taylor himself, a notion that filled me with anxiety and dread. But now I believed I was bound to a living law as a cop, wandering the city, trying to resolve the various disputes and controversies we encountered. I wished I had been bound to the law in my early years wandering the country. It could have saved me so much confusion, so much crime.

The reason is that the law not only preserved a peculiar kind of humanity, it presumed one, even during the times when it could not be felt. In the worst domestic batteries and murders, the law forged some resolution, some justice, even when everything appeared hopeless. In its power to do so, the law seemed to have its origins beyond the miserable, crooked city that gave it a hollow, false life in this courtroom, in this city. In front of this judge in the crooked city, I could for the first time feel the power of this law, could see how badly I needed it in my life. It had an origin in a more powerful, sacred place, one where everyone, even these wrongful conviction zealots, could be forgiven. This courtroom was the first time in my life that I had to admit I just might believe in God after all, and that the law was, for me, the pathway to him, as both a cop and writer.

Standing in front of this judge I would despise if she ruled I had to cough up the emails, this idea was a truly revolutionary notion. It took my mind out of the gutter of vengeance and violence, where, I believed, Taylor and his colleagues lived, and raised the aim of my writing from merely incendiary to something more powerful, something beautiful, even, if I could pull it off. Could I? The judge rummaged through the large stack of my emails, thousands of them. Then she announced she was turning a few of them over to Taylor, the ones dealing with Burge's statement about the reparations, just as I had imagined. Without missing a beat, Taylor asked that the other emails be saved in case they should be released later. The judge refused and then she called for a recess of ten minutes. She made us wait more than an hour, before my cousin and I could finally get outside, away from Taylor, the judge, and the city's goddamn courts.

Chapter 14

HOBLEY APARTMENT

F antasy reigned, as a kind of tyranny. I would have nothing more to do with it unless I could tie it to something tangible, something unequivocally real. I had this sense that I wasn't the only one who felt this need. So one morning I called my friend Wrigley to go with me to the South Side and visit the building that Hobley had set on fire on the 1200 block of East Eighty-Second Street. I picked him up in Logan Square, and we headed south on the freeway.

When Wrigley and I first met in the academy, he was single. Now he was married with three kids, and it was rare when he could get a day off to hang out. But no one knew the burden of this fantasy world I now felt enveloping me and the rest of the city better than Wrigley. In 2005 Wrigley and his partner were leaving a home where they had dropped off a youth on a curfew violation when they heard possible gunshots nearby. They got into their squad car and drove toward the area where they had heard it. As they approached, they observed a van driving the wrong way on a one-way street without the lights on. They followed the vehicle, punching in the plate on the computer. After the information came back, they turned on their lights and pulled the van over. As they did so, two officers in another squad car pulled up behind them, backing up Wrigley and his partner. The two backup officers were from another unit. The man in the van jumped out, yelling that they had no right to pull him over, and that he was an off-duty railroad cop. The officers tried to calm him down. For a moment he did, putting his hands on the van. But then he began fighting with them. He pulled his hands to his waist as the officers struggled with him. He pulled out a gun, two of the officers yelling this fact out to the other officers. The man began firing at all four officers from a short distance.

Wrigley said many times afterward that he could hear the bullets going by his ear. Three of the officers returned fire. Wrigley felt two bullets strike him, one at his heart, which was blocked by his vest, another that struck his arm, traveled upward, and then went out at his shoulder. All told, the man fired seventeen rounds at the officers, who returned dozens of shots, striking him some eighteen times. But in a move that would, in my mind, undermine any claim of misconduct by the police or any conspiracy theory that would arise from the shooting, all the officers ceased firing as soon as the offender ran out of bullets. Two other cops were also wounded in the shooting. Miraculously, none of them were seriously hurt. The offender was charged with four counts of attempted murder. His attorney concocted a defense theory alleging racism, suggesting Wrigley and the other cops pulled over his client and shot him because he was black, a sign of just how deeply ludicrous police corruption theories like those of the People's Law Office had penetrated the imagination of the city.

If the cops attacked the offender because of his race, shot him eighteen times, why did they stop firing when the offender ran out of ammunition? Why did Wrigley and the other officers let him live? And why did he fire seventeen times at them? The first trial resulted in a hung jury, a few jurors buying into the racism fairy tales. At the second trial, the offender was convicted on all nine counts and sentenced to forty years. He lost all his appeals. After the appeals were finished, prosecutors assured Wrigley and the other officers that the case was closed and that would be the end of it. But then Governor Pat Quinn, who had lost a bitter and close race to a Republican challenger, released the offender from prison without explanation just minutes before Quinn left office, without any new evidence supporting such a decision. A governor merely let out, for no reason, a man who shot three cops, for no reason, just as the governor two terms before him, George Ryan, had let out Hobley and three other men from death row in 2003. Wrigley and the other officers had spent nine years waiting for the case to resolve in the courts before Quinn let the offender out, the entire nine years now a complete waste of their lives, serving no purpose. I sat through both trials as much as I could, as the courtroom was filled with the offender's supporters, but only a few cops could trickle in each day to support Wrigley and the other officers. The morning I called Wrigley to visit the Hobley crime scene, we were still reeling from the decision by Quinn, still shocked that a governor could get away with doing such a thing. What must it have been like for the detectives in the Hobley case when Ryan let him out? Quinn's release of the man who shot Wrigley generated little attention from the media, though it was a bombshell story. The way the city was, any story that contradicted the anti-police myth that the PLO and their allies had constructed was simply ignored.

"You got Roscoe?" I asked Wrigley just after he got in the car when I picked him up in Logan Square, Roscoe a nickname for a gun. I had been using this nickname since the academy because it annoyed Wrigley.

"Yes, I have my gun," he said.

"Loaded?"

Wrigley only turned his head toward me with a look of annoyance.

"Ya gotta have bullets in there, ya know. Otherwise, it defeats the whole purpose."

He stared at me.

I pulled out a reporter's notebook, mostly a prop, though I did plan on taking some notes. I also propped a pen above my ear.

"Here's the deal," I said. "We'll act as if we are reporters. I'll say I'm a writer, which is true. Hopefully, they won't ask too many specific questions. If they know we're cops, they won't cooperate and there may even be trouble. If they think we're in the media, they might be cooperative and let us into the building, okay?"

Wrigley nodded. I looked at him more closely. It would be difficult for him to pass for anything besides a cop: short hair, clean shaven, thick belt, very serious in his manner. Certainly not a reporter. Better I should do the talking at first. I turned back to the road, the first time in a while since I had gone to the South Side. As we drove to the Hobley apartment building, both of us fell silent. I could tell Wrigley was lost in his thoughts. Without any conversation between us, I began to ruminate on the strange ways these murder cases had invaded my imagination.

A few days earlier I was working my regular foot beat on Devon, assigned to work an annual carnival for the prolific Orthodox Jewish community living in the district. There wasn't much to the assignment, save standing on the street and nodding at the families when they said hello. I had the transcripts of the Hobley trial on my phone, so I pulled them up and began reading them, and scrolled down to the testimony of various victims trying to escape the flames. One man described hearing the fire, looking out, and seeing the smoke. He went to grab some clothes, touched the handle of the door seconds later, and it was burning hot. That's how quickly the fire was spreading. One woman described being alerted by her son, a heavyset man, who then rushed back toward the flames to alert other family members. He was later found dead, a hero. Such courage. One woman described climbing out the window with her daughter, trying to climb down a drain pipe, but falling onto a car, badly injured. Another older man described the severe burns he received and his long stint in the burn center. As I was reading these accounts, my anxiety grew. I was transported to the scene, and the carnival around me receded from my consciousness. I was back at the fire, reliving it once again.

It was then that two Indian men suddenly ran up to me from across the street, obviously terrified. They could barely speak English, but I heard them say over and over, "Fire, fire." *What the fuck*, I thought. How could I be reading about the Hobley fire and then these two guys run up to me? I looked down at my phone, then back at them. They pointed down the street, and there was a large apartment building, one I knew well, filled with Indian families, flames and smoke pouring out of a top-floor window, just like the fucking Hobley arson, I thought. I ran across the street to the building as I pulled the microphone of the radio close to my mouth.

"2481, emergency. Give me the air."

"2481, you have the air."

"Squad, got a building on fire over here, flames coming out of a top-floor window. Send fire over here."

It was then I realized I didn't know the address. *Dumb fucking ass. How long have you worked this beat?*

"What address?" the dispatcher said.

"Squad send fire to Sacramento and Devon. I'll give you the address in a second. I need some help over here, some other cars."

Already, after just a one-block sprint, I was so winded, I could barely speak coherently into the microphone. My vest was heavy, as were my belt and radio. I held my hat on with one hand. I would have to go into the building right away, start getting people out. I figured I would go toward the fire on the top floor and work down from there. Where was the fucking entrance? Would someone buzz me in? Would I have to break some windows? The imagery of the Hobley arson was still with me. Would I see burning bodies, children, like the cops and firemen witnessed at the Hobley apartment?

"Squad, the address is 3306 West Devon. I'm going inside."

I ran around the building, looking for the entrance. Finally I found it on the west side, near the alley, a strange place for an entrance. Inside the lobby, the door was locked. I rolled my hand down the directory, buzzing dozens of units. Then I looked for something to brace the door open so the firemen and other cops could get in easily. The only object available was a large bench against the wall, so I ran over and grabbed it as the buzzers went off, some asking who it was.

"Police," I shouted, carrying the heavy bench with both arms to the door. "Buzz me in right now."

The door buzzed. I opened it, stuck the bench between the door and frame so the door could not lock, then began sprinting up the flights of stairs, unable to fill my lungs with enough oxygen. There was smoke in the hallways. Doors opened, Indian men, half-dressed, coming out.

"Get out right now. Get your family. Knock on the doors of your neighbors," I shouted, and many of them started doing so.

Now I was on the top floor, but I couldn't tell which door was the one to the fire. Were there already people dead inside, children? Would it be like the pictures of the Hobley victims at the morgue? Furiously I kicked and pounded on the doors, trying to push them open, shouting to ask the people inside if everyone was okay. Then finally one door opened and smoke came billowing out. Inside was an Indian family, gathered about a small kitchen. We were silent for a moment, looking at each other. I spoke first, my radio rattling off announcements of others responding to the scene.

"Is everyone okay?"

"Yes," the Indian man said.

A window was above the sink. The man of the house held a flaming pot in the sink. The flames danced before this window, making it look far worse than it was. He still held the smoldering pan as we looked at each other.

"Squad, slow it down. It's only a small pan on fire," I tried to say over the microphone, but I was laboring too much to breathe. Sweat was dripping from my forehead. My shirt was wet. It took a few attempts. As I tried to speak, I heard the fire department sirens outside.

I went back outside, leaning over a railing along a step up into the building, not able to get enough air. I was so fucking out of shape. Would I have a heart attack? The firemen rushed past me with a bunch of equipment. Coworkers walked up, watched me desperately trying to breathe. I wondered if I had overreacted. Didn't I notice that there was no smoke coming out of any other windows, that not one person was fleeing the building? But that was crazy. Flames and smoke were coming out of one window. That was enough. I still labored to breathe, my mind racing. Reading the Hobley transcripts and then being called to a fire felt as if I were being caught up in a fantastical world I could not escape, one that was toying with me. I leaned over a railing, my chest aching. A crowd had gathered. Part of me wanted to stand on a step in front of the building and address them, raise my hands and explain everything.

"You see, my Indian and Pakistani brothers and sisters, this little kitchen fire was no accident. No sir, not at all. That's not how Chicago works. It was an example of how the city fuses the fantastic and the mundane. Think about it over your tandoori chicken tonight. How could I be reading the Hobley transcripts and then this fire breaks out? What are the chances of that? I can see, brothers and sisters, you do not know what the Hobley arson is. I can see also that many of you do not understand English. You know what, I hadn't thought about that before I began speaking."

I could see their blank stares at me, my deflation.

"Speaking of tandoori chicken," I would say, radically changing directions, "have you tried the chicken at JK Kabab on Rockwell? Holy moly is that stuff good."

But as I stood slightly above the gathering crowd, pulling in air, I kept my thoughts to myself.

Wrigley and I were on the expressway, passing the area where the projects had been and where Anthony Porter was raised. At the time we were heading to the Hobley building, several cities were exploding in riots after the police in other cities had shot offenders or they had died in custody. Despite the violent reactions, most of the shootings were deemed legal. The riots that broke out regardless of the evidence were a sign to many of us in law enforcement that an anti-police hysteria was sweeping the nation. The Hobley arson was, in my mind, a turning point in the long campaign against the police, not only for the city, but for the whole country. The evidence against Hobley was overwhelming. Nevertheless, it was turned into a wrongful conviction. If the police could be vilified in a mass murder case like this one, there was nothing that could stop the wrongful conviction movement. It seemed as if there were a revolution brewing in the country, and that its origins lay in Chicago.

I looked over at Wrigley, who'd been shot twice: the governor let the shooter out of prison without explanation. That rotten, no-good motherfucker. The Porter case, Hobley, the riots throughout the country. So much seemed at stake, not just the legitimacy of a literary movement, nor the city's criminal justice system. It seemed as if the republic itself was being tested, as if the bonds that would hold it together were unraveling rapidly in the wake of a revolution long under way, one that began by magically turning killers into heroes. It was more than that, though. Theirs was a weary revolution, no longer filled with the idealism and enthusiasm of its early years, in the 1960s, one that had lost sight of any deliverance. Their Marxist utopia was long lost, littered with corpses and corruption. Its native proponents seemed to have settled into the habits of destruction for its own sake. The media sucked up to them. The activists were now captains of a corrupt industry they had created, suing the city for millions and millions. Hobley had gotten $7 million. As I drove south with Wrigley—a collection of Hobley crime scene photos in the backseat, photos I would use to guide me through the apartment building if I could get access—I felt the familiar rumblings of my own revolutionary fervor, just as I imagined members of the PLO did in the 1960s. The police were the ones still working the street, on the outside of legitimacy, as the 1960s radicals had once been. In my own outcast condition, the magic of revolution had moved into our camp by telling the whole story of these exonerations like those of Porter and Hobley. For me, it all came back to an apartment building on the South Side of Chicago.

At the same time, I sensed a necessary but dangerous shift in my imaginative life: a move beyond the nonfiction universe I had been living in for more than a decade. Nonfiction was a form that had sufficed to a point, but now proved inadequate—pedestrian even—in the face of the burn patterns that now confronted me. As a writer and cop, I was obligated to follow these patterns to the fantastical places they embraced. Other forms, like fiction, loomed on the horizon for me. I needed the lie of fiction not just for its potential to follow these patterns into the realms of the fantastic, but also as a matter of survival, for the legal attack on me by the PLO would certainly not be the last from the wrongful conviction activists. Soon, I figured, they would entangle me in more traps, at three hundred fucking dollars an hour. This was their method, how they whittled you down. Look at Burge. It took thirty years, but they finally got him in jail. Soon, all my creative energies would be spent in an anxious stew of legal theories, the dreaded phone calls to lawyers who never answered a question unambiguously, the clock always running as they babbled on and on. In fiction, I could hide the truth behind the impregnable wall of deceit that the literary form offered, and thus avoid all legal entanglements. But the deception part scared me, apart from my ignorance of its mechanics and its craft. In nonfiction there was a foothold into the real world, an anchor in a city constructed on such complex layers of deceit and betrayal. This anchor would be gone. I would be floating free and, however unwittingly, I feared being transformed into an agent of the city's corruption, the way so many journalists and students had been bought and sold in the fictions about wrongful conviction cases.

A host of new problems rose up, creating an intense anxiety. I looked over at Wrigley, texting his kid. *Calm the fuck down*, I told myself. Stick with the burn patterns introduced by the detectives, ones rooted in the actual crime scene itself. This was the way to navigate a crooked city. It was, I realized, why I was going to the Hobley apartment building, because it was the epicenter of the city's burn patterns in ways I was only beginning to imagine. In trying to free Hobley, his wrongful conviction attorneys argued endlessly about the origin and path of the fire from his apartment door down the stairs. Hobley's supporters questioned the investigators' claims about Hobley lighting the fire on the first floor after creating a path of gasoline from his apartment door down the steps. But it wasn't just the Hobley crime scene where the burn patterns were obfuscated. The city had been arguing about burn patterns for more than a hundred years, beginning with the Haymarket bombing. In my own time, people argued about who tossed the bomb and if the police got it right. The true burn patterns, therefore, were crucial. They offered up the barest outlines of the city, the skeleton of the city's essential corruption and its methods. They offered up a city constantly vying, constantly engaged in revolutionary plots, as I was. I had become a writer who adopted the perspective of a detective as a literary technique because it would reveal these patterns, this architecture. If I could only show the true burn patterns. I know, I know. Big talk for a guy who didn't even have a publisher anymore, but I just couldn't resist it. I just couldn't.

As we pulled up on Eighty-Second Street, I pointed out to Wrigley the viaduct I had read so much about. That was where Hobley emerged after the fire started and victims began running out of the building and jumping out of windows. I figured he had fled there to wait for the flames and smoke to emerge from his apartment. When he saw smoke and fire pouring out of the entire third floor, he panicked and returned to the building, pretending he himself had escaped. Hobley even helped one victim catch a child who had been tossed from the third floor. I told Wrigley that I had spoken to a woman who was a child at the time of the fire and lived a few doors down. She told me that everyone gathering outside the building was whispering Hobley's name, because the domestic fights between Hobley and his wife were common knowledge around the neighborhood. That, plus the fact that he had survived and his wife and child had not. So even as Hobley milled about the building, trying to look as if he were a victim as well, the people in the neighborhood were already eyeing him. One of the most suspicious things about Hobley's behavior was the fact that he never went to the window below his own apartment and called out for his wife and child. Witnesses spoke about how unemotional he was about losing his family. He did call his

mother, who showed up with her landlady. His mother took
Hobley back to her apartment a few blocks away. But what
man would leave the scene of a fire that had just engulfed his
own wife and child, I wondered. I was telling this to Wrigley,
who was nodding his head.

If anyone could understand false narratives about the
police, it would be Wrigley. That was one reason I brought
him here, I realized. He could understand my need to walk
through the building and physically encounter the location
of this crime. Perhaps, in a way, it was reassuring to him as
well. After watching a governor set free the man who shot
him, similar narratives might provide some perspective on
what happened to him. In the case where Wrigley got shot,
the supporters of the offender concocted many theories
about Wrigley and his coworkers being racist killers, just as
they concocted conspiracy theories about the detectives in
the Hobley case. They even suggested that Wrigley and the
other cops shot each other as part of a plot to cover up their
own alleged attempted assassination of the offender. What a
claim. Who could imagine such a thing? That one of
Wrigley's partners shot him in the chest, inches from the
edge of his vest? When Wrigley was taken to the county
hospital after he was shot, they pulled off his leather jacket. A
smashed bullet—the one that had struck him—matching
the caliber of the offender's gun, fell out on the floor. How
did that get there? A question lingered at Hobley's crime
scene: Would Governor Quinn have set free the man who
shot Wrigley if Governor Ryan hadn't set free Madison
Hobley and three other convicted killers a decade earlier?
Would the governor have done this if there had not been a

precedent, if others hadn't also gotten away with it? Probably not, I concluded. That was another reason I wanted to have Wrigley with me, to show him how he too was connected to this burn pattern. We all were.

We got out of my car, next to the building. It was a lousy neighborhood and we stood out as two white guys. I kept my reporter's notebook in my hand and the pen over my ear. I fingered the pistol on my belt beneath my shirt. Walking by the building, you would never know what had happened here. There were no plaques, no memorials, no paragraph etched in some metal display saying that a mass murder took place here in 1987 and the convicted killer was set free, was then given $7 million. The obscurity of this mass murder struck me again. In 1924 seven men were murdered as part of a gang war in the infamous St. Valentine's Day Massacre. Historians, writers, and journalists had spent decades analyzing every aspect of the massacre, trying to figure out exactly what happened and why. Not so with the Hobley arson. It remained largely unknown, and the narrative about it viciously guarded by its adherents.

I opened my car's back door and grabbed the photographs of the Hobley crime scene. Wrigley had never seen them before. The worst were the ones of children in the morgue—Philip Hobley, for example. The others showed clearly the signs of the intense heat on the upper floors, in the stairwell, and in the Hobley apartment. Wrigley and I stood outside the car. Looking at these photos, we looked back at the building. It looked much the same. The top floors had been engulfed, but the structure and skeleton of the building were not destroyed. We walked around the building, re-creating the night of the fire as best we could. I observed the third-floor windows, the ones people had jumped out of or tossed their children from. There was no grass to soften the landing of those who jumped or fell. A man came out of the building, into the alley. He was middle-aged and looked as if he was on his way to work. I asked if he would mind answering a few quick questions, and he agreed in a friendly manner.

"I'm a writer doing a story on a crime here that took place in 1987—"

"The fire?" he interrupted.

"Yes, the fire. You know about it?"

"Everyone knows about it."

"You didn't by chance live here or in the neighborhood back then?"

"No. My girlfriend lives here."

"You don't know of anyone in the building who lived here the night of the fire?"

"Yeah, there is a woman who was a child back then. She got out the back door," the man said, pointing to it. "But I don't know her number or anything."

I gave the man my phone number in case he ever ran into her. Then I asked him if he would let us into the building. He declined but said the management company was just down the street a few doors and was open.

The only man in the office thought I was a reporter. He agreed to let us into the building. Why, I don't really know. I wondered as we walked back, what he would say if he knew we were both cops. I doubted he would let us in. There was just too much hostility against the police, and the gangs in the neighborhood could be angry with him if they found out he was helping some cops. As he opened the front door, I recalled that this was the door Hobley escaped from after he lit the fire. Probably he knew from the instant he dropped the match on the gasoline-soaked stairs that he had overdone it, that this fire, unlike the one a few days earlier, would be way out of control. He probably heard the powerful whooshing sound, saw it for a moment race up the stairs, thick, black smoke pouring out immediately. Inside I saw another door, one the fire department had to break through because it was locked, the first clue that the offender might live in the building. Just beyond were the stairs, the ones that had burned at such a high heat they crumbled. We paused in the hallway at the bottom, me taking pictures.

It was here I recounted many of the details about the fire, the overwhelming evidence of Hobley's guilt. Wrigley listened closely, so I went deeper into it. I told Wrigley how I had recently tracked Patricia Phiefer, the woman who took in Hobley's wife and child and called the police after he threw a brick through her window. She lived near Hobley's apartment. She was home and awake the night of the arson. She heard the fire trucks go rolling past, the sirens, and she somehow knew. She picked up her phone and dialed Hobley's apartment, but of course it was already too late. Anita Hobley was dead in the apartment, as was the baby, Philip. By the time of the call, the phone was likely melted, along with everything else in the apartment. The line rang and rang. Phiefer grew frantic. She knew Hobley was guilty, just as did Officer Evans, who'd heard Hobley's arson threats the day he came to Phiefer's apartment. Evans called down to

Area 2, where the detectives were interviewing Hobley. The detectives were now certain Hobley was their man.

So what torture were the wrongful conviction attorneys talking about? What coercion? In the imaginations of these wrongful conviction activists, was Evans's case report just a lucky coincidence that bolstered the cops' conspiracy to frame Hobley? Were the detectives so sick and twisted that they would choose to frame a man they did not know, a man who had just lost his own wife and child? Evans's case report was not only key evidence that Hobley was the killer, but that there was no need for coercion whatsoever. But neither Phiefer nor Evans, who would rise to the upper ranks of the police department, could imagine that the fire was only the beginning of a bizarre narrative. They could not imagine that Hobley would be convicted, sent to death row, and then suddenly be released by a crooked governor, himself about to be sent to prison. They couldn't imagine that Hobley would then sue the city and settle for $7 million and that he would be walking around free and rich. I told Wrigley that after Hobley got out, he had several relatives who lived up north in my district, that he was often up there. He obtained medical treatment at St. Francis Hospital in Evanston, where I was born, where we often took victims and inmates needing treatment. He was free as a bird. Wrigley listened to my account carefully. Cops loved hearing these stories, whereas when I told them at a party with my non-cop friends, they listened carefully, but squirmed quite a bit, resistant to the implications behind such a story, then changed the subject. For cops, the Hobley saga made perfect sense.

We went inside the building, to the stairs. These were new. One of the photos of the fire scene shows a fireman standing in front of the collapsed stairwell. But the new one was built in the exact configuration of the old, and the hallways of the floors looked identical as well. I could see what the fire investigators meant by chimney effect. The stairwell was small, rectangular. Smoke and heat would have gone straight up, then out to the floors, the highest floors getting the worst of it. The path of the gas up the stairs and out onto the third floor gave the fire a kind of direction, a pathway, not only revealing Hobley's intent to kill his wife, but also serving as a metaphor of Hobley's rage, a line of fire so focused on getting his wife, it was oblivious to the wider consequences, the killing of his own child and people Hobley didn't know, or barely knew.

Wrigley and I walked up to the third floor. I knew Hobley's apartment was close to the top of the stairwell, but I had never placed it accurately in my mind. There it was just across the stairwell, a few feet. Hobley wasn't going to fuck up this second arson, not like New Year's Eve when a neighbor smelled smoke and put the fire out. This attempt was late at night. The other renters would surely be sleeping and would not smell the smoke in time. Hobley had gotten out of bed, picked up a gas can, and filled it at the gas station down the street. He returned, this time soaking the door and floor outside the apartment, letting some gasoline seep underneath the door, and then he poured a path down the stairs. No small puddle of gas outside the door this time. And if someone opened a door of another apartment, he would hear the door unlocking and have enough time to slip back into the stairwell unseen. I can imagine his building rage against his wife as he poured the gas. *You fucking bitch. I'll be free to do whatever I want.*

Wrigley and I stood outside the door to Hobley's apartment. I couldn't help it. I had to knock. It was a risky move, two white guys knocking on a door of someone in a neighborhood like this. What if they were pissed? What would I ask them?

"Sir, are you aware that a mother and child were burned to death in this apartment in 1987, and the man who did it was sprung from death row and given $7 million?"

Likely whoever lived there knew about the fire. It was common knowledge in the neighborhood. Do you get a break in the rent when two people were burned to death inside? More questions came to mind, ones I would like to ask but never would: "Do you ever have dreams? Do you ever hear voices?"

I looked at Wrigley, then leaned close to his ear and whispered, "We'll just say we are journalists, writing a story about the fire. If they get pissed, we'll apologize and get the fuck out of here."

Wrigley nodded. I knocked meekly three times. There was no answer. I knocked again, harder, but still nothing. In a way, I was relieved. It was so risky. My heart was beating a little bit faster. Wrigley and I were both sweating in the hot hallway. We walked down the hall, the same direction the flames took, past each apartment door. I recognized the numbers from the reports. Many of these people did not make it. Along this floor, firemen had crawled while their coworkers were shooting water on the flames. The ones crawling could not see much at all, but they felt their way, pulling out several bodies. I could never do that. I could never be a fireman. Twice I had been inside buildings that were on fire, banging on doors to get people out. The smoke was not bad. The situation was not dire, but I was coughing and choking on such little smoke and I wanted to get the fuck out of there so bad. Days afterward I was still coughing. Wrigley and I walked back, and then down the stairs to the second floor, walking that floor as well. Then we headed outside again, to the side of the building. This seemed a good time to go over the gas can evidence with Wrigley.

Initially, fire investigators determined that the offender had poured the gasoline outside Hobley's door, then down the stairwell, lit it, and ran. The day after the fire, detectives would return to the building, searching for the can. On the second floor, inside a cupboard of an apartment, they found one. This gas can would provide a rare, temporary victory for the defense, for they, along with the claims that Hobley was abused while in custody, would compel the supreme court to demand an evidentiary hearing. This evidentiary hearing went on for two years, over the course of which Hobley's attorneys would posit a collection of often contradictory theories about the can. For example, they argued that a lab fingerprint report, negative for any fingerprints from Hobley, was not given to them, a sign, they claimed, that prosecutors were covering up evidence of Hobley's innocence. Yet the negative report was cited in numerous documents, including the detective's report. In the changing defense theories about the significance of the gas can, Hobley's attorneys at one point alleged that a cop took another gas can out of the evidence section of the police department and planted it at the crime scene. In order to prove this theory, the defense brought in an offender from another arson who testified that he recognized the gas can planted at the Hobley scene as the one he used in his own crime. Asked how he recognized it, the man said by the tape wrapped around the top of the can. The problem was that this tape had been wrapped around the gas can in the lab, not before, a clear sign that this witness was lying. It was another possible instance of a witness in a wrongful conviction case caught fabricating a story.

The defense theories for the whole Hobley case imply a vast conspiracy by a large group of detectives and prosecutors. In order to plant the gas can to implicate Hobley, several detectives would have had to be in on the plot. That means all of them would have had to agree to frame Hobley for the murder of seven people in less than a twenty-four-hour period. They would have had to agree on the tactics of framing him and the whole story in detail. While it is an assumption in almost every wrongful conviction narrative that the police are acting from an intense racial hatred, how likely is it that the core detectives who push this racist frame-up job would be able so quickly to initiate cooperation among fellow officers, and not just coworkers, but supervisors as well? Are all police so inherently racist and hateful that they would jump on the bandwagon of this frame-up job on such a huge case, one with seven people dead, two of them children? The arguments by Hobley's attorneys paint an evil vision of the entire police department, as if all the detectives were unmoved by their visit to the morgue and the hospital, by the suffering of the injured at the crime scene. How fortunate for these truly evil people that their hastily constructed plot survived so many trials and legal reviews, and all the forensic evidence. And how tough all the officers must have been to hang together through the entire saga of the case. And what a stroke of luck for the corrupt detectives that a probationary police officer, unknown to them, would come forward with a case report describing arson threats by Hobley weeks before he set the fire.

Defense attorneys posited another wild claim in an effort to get Hobley out. They pored over the records of anyone associated with the case and found something suspicious about the key witness, Andre Council, the man who saw up close Hobley purchase the gasoline, then walk toward the apartment where the fire soon erupted. Council, who lived nearby, later saw Hobley at the scene of the fire. Hobley's attorneys found in Council an opportunity to connect the Hobley case directly to Jon Burge. A year after the fire, Council himself was arrested for an unrelated arson that resulted in no injuries. In the course of investigating the arson tied to Council, detectives could not find any evidence against him, and the witness statements against him proved untrue. As the case fell apart, detectives determined to release Council without charges, after clearing their decision with a state's attorney. In a somewhat unusual move, detectives requested that Council be released without waiting for his fingerprints to clear. So the watch commander, Jon Burge, signed off on Council's release. A contributing factor in their decision may have been that Council was known among many of the cops because he was a tow truck driver who frequently pulled impounded cars from the districts to the city's lots. It's also true that attorneys and prosecutors knew that Council was a key witness in the upcoming Hobley case, a fact that may also have compelled them to cut Council a favor by letting him out right away.

But for defense attorneys, this slight favor granted to Council became the foundation of their conspiracy theory that Council was being given a pass for the arson he was arrested for, in exchange for false testimony fingering Hobley. It's an incredible theory to put one's mind around— with so many moving parts, one easily gets lost. How, to begin, did the investigating detectives on the Hobley case transform Council into one of their co-conspirators in the days after the Hobley arson? How did they know he would go along with it? Why would he? And then how did Council, knowing he had this leverage against the cops, get a whole new collection of detectives and officers in another arson case simply to cut him loose?

That wasn't the end of the attempts by the defense to put Council under suspicion. Their conspiracy theory against him expanded. At one point, they alleged that Council was the actual offender in the Hobley arson. The willingness of Burge to set him free without waiting for fingerprints was a sign that Burge and the detectives were covering up for Council's being the true offender, they alleged. It doesn't take much to see the absurdity of this claim. Another witness at the gas station—the owner, Kenneth Stewart—also fingered Hobley at the same gas station. His story mirrored Council's. Yet Stewart was a reluctant witness. He didn't want to get involved, in part because he was afraid of retaliation.

But this theory, so incredibly fantastic, never went anywhere in the courts. Council was never truly a suspect in the Hobley arson. He never even knew Hobley. One wonders: How did he get into the locked building to set the fire? But the willingness of Hobley's attorneys to paint another man as the offender had an eerie ring to it. Isn't that what Northwestern investigators were accused of doing to Alstory Simon in the Porter case? Hadn't Simon been released from prison when prosecutors assailed the "confession" obtained from him by Northwestern investigators? Hadn't a judge declared Simon innocent? Was this shifting of the blame to Council another potential sign that the lawyers and activists of the wrongful conviction movement were willing to pin a murder on the wrong guy in their fanatical crusade against the police and prosecutors? The whole racism angle in the Hobley case became even more impossible as one learned more about the case. The cop, Glenn Evans, who came forward with the arson threats by Hobley weeks earlier, which he had documented in a case report, was black. And Patricia Phiefer, the woman who provided refuge to Anita and her son, and also heard Hobley make the arson threats, was also black.

The judge for two years reviewed all the allegations about the gas can being a smoking gun against the detectives. In the end, he ruled, somewhat disgusted, that it was all a load of shit.

Wrigley and I walked to the west side of the building, where the Hobleys' window was on the third floor. Beneath it, right next to the apartment building, was a small home. Perhaps this was the home from which Hobley called his mother after the fire. We were looking at the photos of the crime scene again, matching them up to where we were standing. Hobley's movements after the fire were uncertain. Some of his story was lies, some of it true. He claimed, for example, that someone gave him a coat, as he said he ran out of the building when the building caught fire. But, since he was the offender, it is more likely that he already had a coat on, and several witnesses, including Andre Council at the gas station, said they saw him wearing a blue peacoat before the fire started. But Hobley told detectives he had been wearing a different coat, the tan one he had on when he went to the station with the detectives. One thing is for sure: at some point after the fire, Hobley called his mother, who lived nearby. I tell Wrigley I'm not sure how many grown men who know that their wife and child were trapped in a flaming building would go to a neighbor's house and call their mother. It's possible they would. Hobley's mother came to him, along with the landlady of the apartment where Hobley's mother lived.

"Why? Why would Hobley's mother bring the landlady over, unless they were close friends?" I ask Wrigley.

He shrugs.

But they weren't close friends, I explain. Quite the contrary, as would be revealed years later.

After Hobley confessed to the crime, the detectives decided to get a warrant to search his mother's apartment for the clothes Hobley was wearing at the scene of the fire. Once again, one has to pause and consider the significance of the detectives even getting the warrant. If they were framing

Hobley, why were they being so circumspect in their investigation? Why would they bother getting a warrant? Were the detectives so brilliant in their framing of Hobley that they thought out such minute details as getting a warrant for evidence they knew did not exist, just to make their investigation look more legitimate? Now that would be some brilliant detectives, able to think so clearly in such a short period of time, under such immense pressure. But that's not what truly happened. Hobley had suspiciously handed them a bag of clothes when they first met him at his mother's house. The ambulance drivers who came to Hobley's mother's apartment to take Hobley to the hospital said that they saw him rummaging through his clothes, changing them. The witnesses at the crime scene contradicted Hobley's claims about what he was wearing. And then there was the infamous bath at his mother's house, a clear sign that he was washing away any remnants of the arson. Who takes a bath late at night after his child and wife were burned in a fire? The detectives weren't framing anyone. They wanted to build as strong a case as possible, so they returned the next day with a search warrant. Likely there was gasoline on his coat, as Hobley carried the gas can several blocks and poured it down the stairs. They wanted to collect it as evidence. But when the detectives went back with a warrant to Hobley's mother's apartment the following day, they could not find this coat. Where was it? Here one has to pause and consider the conspiracy theories by Hobley's attorneys. If the detectives were willing to plant a false gas can, as the attorneys later asserted, why didn't they plant a coat with gasoline on it in a dumpster or in an alley near his mother's apartment?

But they didn't, and the question remains: Why didn't the detectives find the coat at Hobley's mother's house? The answer emerged years later, when two retired ATF agents working as private investigators returned to the apartment during an investigation of the case in preparation for Hobley's lawsuit against the city after he was pardoned. The landlady still owned the building, but the Hobleys had moved out. The agents knocked on the door of the landlady and were welcomed in. The landlady told them a story that cleared up everything. The night of the fire, she told the retired agents, Hobley's mother had brought a bag of clothes to the landlady's apartment and told her to hide them or they would kill her. The landlady told the two investigators that she was too frightened of the Hobleys to argue, so she took the clothes, among them a blue peacoat, and hid them. Now that the Hobleys were gone, she could come clean.

Wrigley and I snap a few more pictures, walk around a little more. We get into my car and head over to the gas station where Hobley bought the gas for the fire, but we aren't talking much. Wrigley knows the power of the wrongful conviction crowd. They got the man who tried to murder him out of prison. They are going after me, I'm certain. First, it was taking me to court, getting a judge to rule I had to turn over emails from Jon Burge. Certainly the closer I get to the truth in the Hobley case, the more they will come after me. I feel my rage coming up. I find myself degenerating into a chronic diatribe, a vicious cursing against the city. I've seen it in Wrigley as well, seen it in all cops. The last I've heard about Hobley is that he changed his name and moved to North Carolina, a wealthy man after the city gave him $7 million. That motherfucker. He got out of the arson, walked right out of death row, just like Porter. The wrongful conviction activists created this fantastical world about these crimes, a world obliterated by looking closely at the crime scene and the investigation of it. I feel doom cover over me, regret I ever came to the city, and have the sense that no matter what I do with these murders, I am throwing my life away. I too am burning, burning silently as Wrigley and I head north again, away from Hobley's apartment building, the very center of the city's burn patterns.

Chapter 15

THE RIVER

I was heading southbound through the city in my car, early on a summer morning, heading downstate to the Danville State Prison. I had put off this trip for more than a year. I could only visit the prison on a weekday, at the request of the inmate I was going to visit. He was a convicted killer and rapist. As I pulled out onto Interstate 55, I reminded myself that it would be best not to let anyone at the prison know that I was a cop. It could be trouble for the inmate I was going to see, Darryl Simms, and I didn't want to sit in the prison waiting area with people knowing who I was. Should I tell the corrections officers? Better play that by ear. Already, an anxiety was coming over me, one I couldn't fully explain. Part of it was certainly from the thought of spending an afternoon with a man who had been on death row. But there was something more to it, a growing sense that prison loomed for me, as well. I could see in my paranoia—every cop could—that somehow I could end up in the system, but even as a writer I sensed an imaginative box closing in on me, felt that I would pay a high price for rejecting the city's crooked mythology about wrongful convictions.

It was a three-hour drive to Danville, but it would be much longer for me because, in this growing anxiety, I could not stomach traveling the interstate with all the billboards bombarding me. It would be a violation of the solitude I wanted before arriving there, so I picked out country roads beforehand that passed through miles of farmland and small towns. On those roads, I would roll the window down and smell the earthy smells, look at the lonely farms, recall how I used to travel these roads when I was younger, hitchhiking. At one point, I would stop in at one of these towns and get a big country breakfast and read the local paper. I loved reading local newspapers. But now I was just driving into the South Side of Chicago, past so many landmarks of the murders I had researched, many of them that had become cases against Jon Burge and his men. To my left, Anthony Porter had gunned down Marilyn Green and Jerry Hillard. A few miles later, to my left again, Hobley had set the fire.

The inmate I was going to see, Darryl Simms, had been convicted in 1985 of raping and killing a woman. He stabbed her twenty-five times as her three children slept in another bedroom. Her body was discovered by her husband when he came home from work. After Simms was found guilty, prosecutors brought forth three more women who said they were raped at knifepoint in the months before Simms had murdered the victim. With such a brutal crime and such a lengthy record, the judge gave Simms the death penalty. Simms joined a host of other men on death row, all of them fighting to stave off their executions. One of these men on death row with Simms was Anthony Porter, who would walk out of death row in 1999 and run into the arms of Professor David Protess. With the cameras clicking, Porter would pick up Protess in his embrace, lifting him off the ground. Another inmate on death row at this same time was serial killer John Wayne Gacy, who murdered at least thirty-three young men and hid their bodies in the crawl space under his home. Gacy was executed while Simms was on death row, Gacy's final words being "Kiss my ass." The lethal injection took some twenty minutes to take effect. Still another man on death row with Simms was Madison Hobley.

This collection of death row inmates provided a road map of the wrongful conviction movement and its ascending power not only over the city's public institutions, but over the collective imagination of the city, and beyond. In freeing Porter, wrongful conviction activists had undermined the prosecutor's office, for the evidence was clear that prosecutors knew Porter was guilty and Simon was innocent, but they went ahead with Porter's exoneration nevertheless. In Chicago-speak, this meant that the wrongful conviction movement essentially "owned" the prosecutors, that they had these elected officials in their back pocket. A second sign of their growing power was Governor Ryan's willingness to pardon Porter, then for Ryan to use that case as justification for pardoning Madison Hobley and three other men in 2003, without any new evidence. These exonerations signified that the movement now "owned" the governor's office as well, quite an accomplishment for a once ragtag collection of radicals in the 1970s. But the Hobley case took the movement

beyond the mere limits of state corruption, into the realm of
the national. After Hobley was set free, federal prosecutors
began to take a long look at the case, seeing that something
horribly crooked had taken shape. They considered new
charges against Hobley. But at the same time, the claims
against Jon Burge, pushed relentlessly in the local media,
intensified. Despite all the accusations hurled against Burge's
men, none had been criminally charged. The two cases,
Burge and Hobley, ended up on the desk of federal prosecutors, the legal case against Hobley overwhelming, and the
media pressure by the wrongful conviction activists in the
Burge cases calling for federal criminal charges. So federal
prosecutors had to make a decision: Burge or Hobley.

And so they did.

One morning at his Florida home, Burge—who had
never missed one court date, had responded to every
subpoena, every call for evidence, had shown up for every
deposition—was awakened to loud knocking on his front
door. Wearing only his underwear and a T-shirt, Burge arose
from his bed and answered the door. He discovered a collection of federal agents gathered outside, many of them
wearing ninja-type uniforms, armed with rifles. They burst
in and began searching his home, regularly calling out
"clear" as they went into each room. Clear of what, one
wonders. What did the Feds think they were going to find in
his home? Hostages? Bomb-making equipment? An arsenal
of weapons? What a transformation. I recalled their antics
against those who opposed them in the criminal justice
system, the fact that thirty years earlier, the wrongful conviction activists and their attorneys were under FBI

surveillance. Many of the agents believed that one member of the Weather Underground, Bernardine Dohrn, was the bomber of a San Francisco police station, killing a police officer. Other members had flown to communist countries, met with the leaders there, and plotted the violent overthrow of the country. They stockpiled explosives and bomb-making equipment. Some would eventually murder police officers. Some would flee to Cuba. Now federal authorities were responding to these former fugitives' narrative about the police, knocking on the door of Burge's home with ninja-clad agents, ignoring, in their efforts, the monumental evidence that Hobley was an arsonist who had killed seven people.

"You guys watch too much television," Burge told them, as one of the lead agents announced they had a warrant for his arrest.

Clearly, this manner of arresting Burge was for show, to appease the media and the wrongful conviction hysteria, both of which were calling for Burge's head. One agent, an older one, stood outside the home, refusing to take part in the "arrest," the look of disgust on his face obvious. Burge was handcuffed, processed, then released on bond a few hours later. The Feds could have easily contacted Burge's lawyer and told him to bring Burge in. They could have called him and told him they were coming. In any case, the Feds made their choice between Hobley and Burge. They pursued a criminal case against Burge and let Hobley go free. When the Feds announced the indictment of Burge, the city settled with Hobley's attorneys for $7 million.

The arrest of Jon Burge was more than just a legal and political transformation. It signified a cultural transforma-

tion as well, for the indictment of Burge intensified the
merging of the magical and the real, confirming with the
force of law that all these killers were victims and the police
were thugs. It was the city's own Cuban revolution, an electrifying transformation. In a fervor of any revolutionary close to
victory, the journalists, academics, and students all operated
under the notion that Burge and his men were torturers and
racists. Every cop was now tainted with the accusations
about a racist conspiracy within the department, from the
lowest patrolman to the superintendent, even the mayor. It
was so satisfying, so revolutionary, that in the frenzy of
Burge's arrest not one Chicago journalist, many of whom had
graduated from Northwestern University's Medill School of
Journalism, took a look at the clear evidence that Hobley was
guilty of the mass murder. And there was an unacknowl-
edged, twisted sentiment that permeated the media's investigations and every sentence they wrote about Burge: Who
cares? The revolution is more important.

Burge's trial began. In the middle of it, one of the federal
prosecutors walked up to Burge's attorney. He casually and
offhandedly said he had come across some documents that
he figured Burge's attorney would want. Burge's attorney
went through them, finding, to his amazement, a report from
federal investigators about a 2008 visit to Darryl Simms in
prison. Simms had sent the federal investigators a letter
saying he had important information about Madison Hobley.
The investigators came to visit him. In their interview with
Simms, he told the investigators that Hobley repeatedly
confessed to setting the fire. Simms said Hobley admitted to
the police that he had, in fact, confessed. He told Simms he

did not intend to kill his child. Simms told investigators that in all the time that Simms and Hobley discussed the arson while on death row, Hobley never claimed the police abused him. This report, given to Burge's lawyers at the beginning of the trial, sent them into a frenzy. They requested a delay in the trial so they could depose Simms, but the judge rejected it. To Burge's attorneys, Simms's statements undermined the criminal case against Burge, for Hobley was pardoned by the governor. Simms's statements reinforced Hobley's guilt in setting the fire. It added to the ever-increasing evidence that Hobley had set the fire. It also lent more credence to the fact that he had not been abused and that he had confessed. Taken together, Hobley's statements to Simms were more evidence that cast a dark shadow on the entire federal criminal case against Burge. There was never any significant evidence that any detectives had abused Hobley. There wasn't even a clear motive for why they would. What was becoming clear in Simms's statements was the fact that Hobley was guilty and that his exoneration was the real crime, not any actions by the detectives. Simms's statements became even more compelling given the trial strategy of the federal prosecutors against Burge. The prosecutors never called Hobley to testify in Burge's trial. How could the key figure in the narrative to convict Burge of torture not even be called to the stand? It was a chilling sign that even prosecutors knew Hobley could not survive cross-examination, just as Hobley had not been able to survive the inquiries of detectives in the interview room after the fire, as detectives weighed the emerging evidence against the account Hobley provided. Simms's buried statement was, in the mind of

Burge supporters, a sign of just how far federal officials were willing to go to generate an official narrative against Burge to secure a criminal conviction, any conviction.

And then there was the media silence over Simms's story about Hobley. One key element in the entire wrongful conviction narrative was the willingness of activists in the movement to buy in to the claims of a convicted killer, often with a long violent rap sheet and established gang affiliations, a narrative in which the convicted man had everything to gain and nothing to lose. Yet no one in the media was willing to listen to the convicted killer Darryl Simms about Hobley. In the entire quest to convict Burge, not one journalist had ever visited Simms to hear his story, even though Simms's account bolstered the evidence and the verdicts against Hobley so completely. It was just like no one had bothered to interview Hobley's mother's landlady, who told investigators that she had hidden a bag of clothes after the fire because, she said, she was threatened by Hobley's mother if she didn't comply. One wonders how many journalists would have traveled to Danville to hear Simms if he were making accusations against Burge or any Chicago cop.

I had not reached the exit for the country roads. Billboards still filled the spaces along the interstate, as if they were shouting at me. I turned down the radio, weary of the noise. The day would be filled with various forms of hostility and guardedness. I rolled up the windows all the way, turned on the air. Doing so seemed to make it easier to think clearly. An anxiety lingering in the back of my mind moved to the forefront. At the same time I began researching and writing about wrongful conviction cases years earlier, I developed several maladies, including an on-the-job back injury that resulted in years of crippling pain and ultimately a spinal fusion. During that time, I experienced for the first time panic attacks. I would awaken suddenly at night, get up to use the bathroom, and then an attack would begin. For days afterward I would be tortured, anxious I would have another. During these attacks, I felt a chilling evil force in the world surrounding me and smothering me. Most of all there was claustrophobia, a desire to get out of any enclosed room. These panic attacks remained always on the periphery of my consciousness, as if they were communicating something real, truthful even, and were waiting for the appropriate time to move to the forefront and assert themselves. Being in an enclosed place, unable to get out, often initiated an attack. The notion now of going inside a prison, therefore, made me especially anxious.

These panic attacks seemed connected to my investigation of the wrongful conviction cases like Porter's and Hobley's. As this panic moved into my imagination, I felt as if I could see the murders with greater sympathy, clarity, and yes, even poignancy. Sounds and images of crime scenes came alive. I could imagine the dwellings where they took place, the silence in the rooms after the offender fled, what it was like when the responding cops first entered the room. When detectives told me that Jerry Hillard, one of Anthony Porter's murder victims who was shot fatally in the head, was snoring in the last moments of his life on the bleachers next to the pool in Washington Park, I felt I could see it so clearly.

I could see the people fleeing the park. And the murder
scenes got worse the deeper I dug into the wrongful conviction movement. Hobley's arson became clear to me, the roar
of the fire, the voices of people yelling to get out, the last
moments of Anita Hobley, who must surely have known this
was the handiwork of her husband as she was burned alive. I
felt as if the panic attacks allowed me to see the city's corruption and crime with an authenticity I had always sought. But
at what cost? The attacks were more than I could manage,
and I sensed they were always trying to reassert themselves
the closer I got to the murders, and to the murderers themselves. Panic attacks also broke the entire world into a grand
duality between the outside world and inside. At the peak of
a panic attack, I would desperately seek to go outside of
whatever building or car I was in. Many late nights I walked
out to my backyard, which was a private beach on Lake
Michigan, to stare at the lake and get hold of my mind again.
Now I was moving in the opposite direction, going from rural
farmlands to a prison. I felt the familiar anxiety emerging as
I got closer to my meeting with Darryl Simms, my heart rate
picking up, sweat forming. *I am fifty years old*, I thought, *going
to talk to a death row killer on my day off*, and I wasn't really
sure I could pull it off without a full-fledged panic attack.

Most cops would visit inmates through an established proce-
dure that would bring the prisoner to them in an interview
room. I was going as a civilian and would be treated like
everyone else. I would have to undergo the background
check, the searches, the same procedures I myself had

performed on so many gang members I'd arrested. The duality between the outside world and being captive inside a prison stirred my anxiety even more. The sense that I had become a criminal came over me again, as it had for the last five years I'd been looking into these murders. And I was a criminal. I was going against a movement that had transfixed the city for thirty years and had the force of the law behind it. Going covertly into the prison added an unpleasant, foreboding realism. The prospect that Jon Burge and his men were innocent of torturing anyone, as I often suspected, haunted me. I worried that the same thing would be done to me as a writer. And yet, I could not walk away from this story. It held me, even in the panic attacks.

Now that I was out of the city, I turned off my air conditioner, rolled down the windows. It was beautiful but insufficient. Today I needed something more than a good country breakfast and the landscape of country farms. And to describe what I needed—to be more honest about my state of mind—I needed fiction again, but I could not, as yet, find a way to it. It seemed that only through fiction could I honestly capture the real nature of my emotional life, moving beyond this romantic twaddle about farmland. I needed something visceral, more elemental and base than a soothing rural landscape. A fictional character could address a desire to stop at some small-town massage parlor along the way to enjoy the delights of a young masseuse. The image came to me. The scent and curves of a woman were a welcome contrast to the sterile, institutional world of the prison I would face later in the day, talking to a former death row killer. I could let my fictional character open up about the thought of a rubdown, the slow disrobing of the masseuse after prices were negotiated, the soft skin, the vocal admiration of her various physical gifts. What if she were truly game, if she enjoyed her work? The lustful talk. How far would she would go? The images danced across the imagination of my fictional character, and then, I confess, mine, her breasts as she leaned over me, stroking her smooth back, sliding downward, culminating in her bent over the table with my fictional character having her.

The signal on my cell phone became sporadic, and I couldn't consistently see the maps of the roads I was taking. Some of the roads turned out to be gravel, so I had to reverse, get back on the paved road, and search for another. The day wore on, and when I finally found the road that would go right into Danville, I stayed on it until I came upon a little town with some restaurants and gas stations. Here I would gas up, use the restroom, then get that country breakfast. Since my phone wasn't working, I figured I'd ask the attendant, an Indian man standing at the register talking on his cell phone, how far I was from Danville. But he remained on the phone, so I headed into the store's restroom. On the floor near the bowl were several dead roaches. There was only a little soap left in the dispenser. There were smear marks of dirt on the floor and the walls. After finishing, I walked through the store looking for water and peanuts, the attendant still jabbering away on his phone. Most of the items for sale were still in their boxes with only the tops cut off, and the store was as dirty as the restroom. Outside the window of the store, I could see down the street to a Shell station, busy with activity. I should have gone there. I put my peanuts and water on the counter, looked straight at the attendant to let him know I had a question, but he kept speaking on the phone.

"Excuse me," I said.

He looked at me, the phone under his chin.

"Can you tell me how far I am from Danville?"

"Dan what?" he said in a strong accent.

"Danville. How far to Danville?"

He leaned into the phone and obviously asked the person on the other end the same question in his native language, but that person did not seem to know either.

"Brother," I said. "Danville. How far to Danville, the next big town?"

He put the phone down and reached for a map and began unfolding it.

"Ah, forget it," I said. "How much do I owe you?"

"Three dollars," he said.

The last time I had been to Danville prison was several years earlier on a failed attempt to interview Alstory Simon. Paperwork problems meant that we never got past the intake room for visitors, the long drive there and back a complete waste of time. I was afraid the same thing would happen today. In the parking lot, I made sure there was nothing in my car that could be construed as a weapon, no fugitive bullets that had fallen from my police bag. I double-checked that my gun was not in the trunk. That would be a dumb-shit move. Then I made my way across the parking lot, the sun beating down.

There were prison employees, mostly corrections officers, walking toward the same door, and a few families, likely also visiting someone. Already I looked and felt out of place. There was the prison before me, thousands of men locked up. In the course of my career, some of my arrests were these inmates. Would they recognize me when I walked through?

I remembered from my last visit how gruff the staff could be. The older man working there handed me a bunch of paperwork. I saw that they were going to check me for warrants and what-not. They wanted the information on my car. I did not know about all the background checks, but it made sense. In this process, I was afraid something would come up indicating I was a cop and one of the officers would announce it in the waiting area, everyone suddenly looking at me. Then, when we went into the prison, the word would spread, and they would know Simms was talking to a cop. One question on the form asked what I did for a living, so I put "writer." "Relationship to inmate" was another question, so I put "interview," then I handed it back. I sat down again. The room filling up with more visitors, many of them gang members covered in tattoos.

Some guy walked in for a visit but found out the inmate was at another prison. He held up a card and said it had twenty dollars' value on it, but would sell it for ten. It was a card you needed to buy items from the vending machines. I remembered then how important vending machines were for inmates. I should have one of these for Simms, as I was sure he would want something and if I couldn't buy him anything, it might end the interview right there. So I pulled out a ten-dollar bill and handed it to the man, putting the card in my top pocket.

I heard the corrections officer call my name, mispronounced.

"You have to state your relationship to the inmate. 'Interview' isn't good enough," he said.

"Well, I don't know him."

"Well, why are you visiting him?"

"I'm writing a book."

Everyone in the room looked up at me.

"Well, put down 'acquaintance' then. You have to have something in there or you can't go in."

He rudely flung the clipboard under the bulletproof window, and I changed it, then went back and sat down.

Groups of people were steadily called back into the prison. Soon they called me. I was taken to a little room where the same corrections officer put on some gloves. Here goes, I figured. He told me to put my arms out, then began patting me down, as I have done thousands of times to suspects. He pulled out my pockets and told me I could take nothing into the visiting room save the vending machine card. He repeated this twice and looked me in the eye when he said it. Everything else would go into a security locker, and I could retrieve the contents on the way out. Next I sat down and took off my shoes and socks, which he went through.

What the fuck, I thought. *I'll try to break the ice.*

"How many years you got on?" I said.

"Twenty-five," he said.

"I work for the Chicago Police. I'm also a writer. Just here to interview someone."

Silence. The ice grew thicker. It was a bad move.

"You will be escorted to the visiting area. You can't talk to anyone and you must follow your escort closely. Understand?"

"Yes, sir."

Out we went into the general population, down several hallways toward a large cafeteria, outside of which was a desk with other officers where my escort signed me in. As he did so, I fingered the vending machine card in my top pocket. I suddenly noticed there was another card in the pocket, the card of an attorney I had spoken to a few days earlier. I had absentmindedly transferred it to this pocket earlier that morning. *Motherfucker*, I thought. What would this corrections officer do if he knew I had brought something in? Should I just ignore it or fess up? It looked as if I would be searched again in front of this desk. Better fess up, I thought. I nodded to the officer and handed him the card.

"I'm very sorry, sir, but I just found this in my pocket."

He glared at me with what seemed a clear hatred. He could get in trouble for missing something so obvious. I looked down. He reached out for it and took it, saying quietly, but with a kind of fury, "I asked you if you had anything more in your pockets."

"I know. I screwed up. I'm sorry."

He just glared at me. I wanted to get the hell out of there. I wanted to be walking down bustling streets with restaurants and people walking about. I wanted to be riding around in a squad car with the windows down, telling jokes with my partner and talking shit. I wanted to be free. The door to a large cafeteria opened up, filled with round tables that had four chairs at each one. Already at several of these tables were inmates with their visitors, some playing board games, others just chatting. The inmates had to remain seated, but the visitors could get up and go to the vending machines. If you had to use the bathroom, you had to wait for a corrections officer to escort you right into the toilet. What a nightmare, I thought, if you had to take a dump. The corrections officer started telling me a bunch of rules I didn't clearly catch, then told me to head to table C4. I looked around. *What the fuck*, I thought. *Where the hell is C4?* He turned away and began talking to someone else. I began walking down the aisle of the cafeteria, looking for any markings on the tables, but could see only that at each one was painted the letter "I" and the letter "V" across from it, meaning, I would later learn, inmate and visitor. So I just stood there in the middle looking back at the corrections officer sitting as his desk. Finally, he saw me and pointed angrily to a table.

"That one right there," he said.

I could imagine how tough their job was, but this treatment was getting to me. *Keep your mouth shut*, I said to myself. *Someday you might be living here.* I sat at one of the chairs, alone at my table as the room filled up with more visitors. Every few minutes, an inmate, escorted by an officer, would appear at the entrance, then meet with some family or girlfriend at a table. The minutes rolled on without Simms appearing. I wondered if the corrections officers were messing with me because I fucked up so much. Then I wondered if Simms, who had once been on death row, was kept in a higher security area that required more processing to move about. Perhaps, I considered, he had changed his mind, or he had been fucking with me from the outset, trying to screw over some cop, and this trip would have been in vain. My spirits sank and my anger rose. What a wild-goose chase this was turning out to be. The room grew noisier. It was going on forty-five minutes since I arrived in the room.

I recognized Simms when he came in, tall, strong, muscular, well groomed. He came over and we shook hands. As I sat down, there was a pressure in my head, a sign of an anxiety attack lingering there. Around us all the tables were filled with many gang member inmates and their visiting families. Simms would either talk or bullshit me, so I just starting asking questions about being on death row with Hobley. There was, he said, a collection of killers in the unit who had been arrested in Area 2, where Burge worked. They had, according to Simms, gotten together on a regular basis on the pretense that they were studying the law about their cases. But in reality, he said, they were actually working together to claim they were tortured, as a means of getting out, just as Porter had. Hobley, said Simms, was unlike any other inmate. He had no criminal record. He stayed by himself, was shy. Simms said Hobley approached Simms because Simms knew about the law. They became friends and spent a great deal of time together. Simms said that Hobley often admitted to setting the fire and never claimed he had been abused by the police. Even up until his last few days in the prison, Simms said, Hobley had admitted to setting the fire. After

Hobley got out, Simms said he never heard from Hobley again. Simms also expressed doubt about the innocence of the other men who had been pardoned by Ryan at the same time Hobley was.

Now I just wanted to get out of there. Earlier I had offered to buy Simms some food from the vending machines. He said no. But now Simms suddenly said he would take me up on the offer. I got up, walked through several aisles of tables where people were talking, and bought him a sandwich, some chips, something to drink. Simms ate the food slowly, and began telling me about his own case, which I did not want to get in to. He asked about my plans with the Hobley case, and I told him, "Right now, only to write a book about it, but I was hopeful that some authorities would take a look at what had happened in this case." It was then that Simms hinted that, with his cooperation on the case, perhaps his sentence could be shortened and he could get out. The thought of Simms wandering free again filled me with even more anxiety.

"I don't know about that. All I do is follow the evidence as best I can," I said. "I am not working on your case."

"I understand," he said, nibbling on his sandwich.

Much of the rest of the conversation I ignored. He was going on about his case. Simms had seen many people walk out of death row. But his crimes had taken place in another county, not Chicago. As he ate, my mind went back to the Burge trial. Burge's attorneys frantically tried to get Simms on the witness stand after the judge rejected their request for a delay. But Simms wouldn't testify. The reason, he said, was that he claimed he had been the victim of abuse by Area 2

detectives, not Burge, many years earlier when he still lived
in the city. Simms claimed officers had sicced a dog on him
during an arrest. I didn't know what to make of this claim.
Simms received some kind of settlement from the incident,
he said, but it was also possible in my mind that he wouldn't
testify because he wouldn't ruin the Burge mythology that
was being used to get so many prisoners out. It would be a
tough life for any convict who killed this golden goose.
Simms was brought back and forth from downstate as
Burge's attorneys worked to get him on the stand during the
trial, but in the end, he would not budge and would not
testify. I wondered what Simms's testimony would have done
in the case. Jury polling indicated there was a lot of doubt
among the jury. Would Simms's testimony have turned it in
Burge's favor?

As Simms went on about his case, I remembered that I
had gone to Burge's 2010 trial at the tail end, after he had
been found guilty. I sat in the gallery, listening to the mob of
activists, academics, and lawyers rant about what an evil
person Burge was. From that point until now in the prison,
my mind had changed about Burge and the detectives. I
wasn't convinced they tortured anyone. If I was right, what
must it have been like for Burge to sit through his trial, for all
the cops who had worked with him to watch this travesty
unfold? Once I had agents and publishers seeking me out. As
soon as I began writing about wrongful convictions, they all
headed for the hills. Then my research had been subpoenaed and a judge actually forced me to turn it over to the
likes of Flint Taylor. Now I was sitting in prison, listening to
Simms tell me about his murder. The prison walls pressed

down on me. I put my mind outside them, the image of me walking on the grass in the parking lot to my car, then driving north with the windows open and all the lonely, beautiful old farms, and all the memories of wandering places like this when I was young and felt so much possibility, and put away the horrible brooding sense that being in this prison was somehow fateful in my own life.

Simms eventually signaled it was time for him to go back to his cell. We walked to the corrections officer in the front, waiting for our escorts. It was an interminable ten minutes. Simms began joking with other inmates. At one point, he looked over at me and nodded, then introduced me to one, an older white guy who looked like a sex offender. That was the last thing I wanted to do: talk to another inmate. The guy asked me how I was doing. Finally, my escort came. Simms and I shook hands, and I headed out of the visiting room. They took me back to the intake room. I assumed, naively, that I would only have to tell them I was leaving and they would give me my ID. It was the same gruff old-timer there. I waved, said I was going.

"Sign out," he said, handing me a clipboard with all the names of visitors on it.

My heart started racing because I knew I had never filled out this log when I came in. The confusion over my relationship with Simms on the intake form had distracted them. The way this guy demanded I sign out made it seem as if this log was a crucial policy.

"I don't remember signing this," I said meekly, as I

rummaged through the names, knowing I would never find mine.

"You did. No one goes in without signing the visitor log," he said.

Motherfucker, I thought. This could be a huge clusterfuck. They might want me to stay to do some kind of investigation. I looked at the door outside, thinking, insanely, about making a break for it. But they would chase me and take me down in the grass, handcuffing me and bringing me back. The officer, fed up with my inability to find my name, snatched the clipboard back from me and began poring over the names.

"How the hell did you get into this place without signing in?"

Clearly he was already trying to pin the fuck-up on me. But it was his job to make sure I signed in and out. He had missed the card in my top pocket on the way in. Now this. He was making me look like the transgressor.

"I don't know."

He threw it down and walked over to a phone and began making calls. Soon, I figured, some investigators or bosses would come out and lead me back into the prison to document the whole thing. I would have to explain I was a cop, that I was a writer, and about the case I was working on. It would be ridiculous. Perhaps they would charge me with some kind of infraction, call my supervisors in Chicago. Perhaps it would be determined that I had entered the prison unlawfully. As anxious as I was becoming, I wanted to curse out the old man. It was his job to make sure I signed it, not mine. I didn't know anything about their fucking procedures.

He was on the phone, waving his hands and speaking in a loud voice. He hung up, made another call. *Goddamn it*, I thought. Then he hung up and walked over. I waited for him to tell me I had to stay.

"Get out of here" was all he said, waving his hand.

Go fuck yourself, I thought, but he didn't have to tell me a second time. I walked out into the heat of the summer day, taking deep breaths, waiting for the anxiety to recede. I cut across the pavement on the grass toward my car, my sweet, sweet car with a radio in it. I retrieved my cell phone from the trunk where I had hidden it and headed north.

About an hour later, I came across a park along the banks of the Kankakee River. I pulled over and parked, walked to the edge, and sat down on a tree stump. It was a lovely, slow-moving river, lined with homes and cabins. We were a few miles outside of Kankakee proper, which made perfect sense. It made sense because Kankakee was the home of Governor Ryan, who had freed Hobley shortly before Ryan himself was sentenced to prison. Anthony Porter, also pardoned by Ryan, had also moved to Kankakee for a while after his exoneration. Porter got into a fight with his girlfriend and sliced her face up with a broken beer bottle, leaving a gash requiring some forty stitches. The media gave full voice to the claims of his supporters that Porter's violent behavior was due to his wrongful conviction, not his violent criminal nature. He never served a day in prison for the attack.

Clouds had been rolling in. Now a drizzle started with the threat of heavier rain. I picked up some stones and tossed them into the water, watching the ripples. Why was it that the closer I came to understanding what truly happened in these cases, the more my life seemed to go astray? This was perhaps the most intense sign of the city's corruption, its ability to ruin anyone who got too close. Burge was convicted and Hobley got off scot-free, wealthy even. I looked out into the middle of the river where the rain was causing small ripples and saw something. It looked stiff, half-floating, half-sinking, as if it were lifeless but at the same time able slightly to resist the force of the current. Like the time that apartment fire broke out when I was reading the Hobley transcripts, there now seemed a strange merging together of my imagination pondering these murder cases and the world around me. I stood up, believing the thing floating was a body. It slowly moved closer to me. It was dark, perhaps a black person. Was that hair? Was it Marilyn Green, the woman shot by Anthony Porter? Was that an arm still raised clutching her neck where the fatal bullet entered? Marilyn's body slowly bobbed and weaved in the water, coming closer to me. So I stood quietly, the rain gently falling. Marilyn seemed to be willfully moving toward me, as if she wanted to speak to me. I felt as if she wanted to tell me I had it just right, as if she were coming toward me to encourage me to keep telling the story, to find a publisher somehow. And then, suddenly, Marilyn's body rolled like an old log, half water soaked.

I was about to sit down again, try to figure out what was happening to me, when I spied other floating objects in the river, floating like bodies down the river. In the quiet of the river and the rain, I recalled that we were downriver from

Chicago, that any debris or artifacts in the water may very well have begun there. A gust of wind rose up and the rain fell a little harder. I looked again at the river. There was little Philip Hobley floating next to his larger mother, both moving closer to me. I liked the notion of these murder victims ending up in this quiet river, as if this water could soothe the burning of their wounds, even after all these years. The river suddenly seemed to me a midpoint between all things real and imaginary. Images of all the horrors I had seen as a cop arose in my mind, the dead children, the gunshot victims, the mangled bodies of traffic crash victims, the rat-infested apartments, brains on sidewalks. What I had experienced as a police officer was much less compared to what the detectives from the 1980s had seen, many of whom had to endure the sight of their own coworkers shot dead. I remained silent, steadfastly watching the parade of bodies come down the river.

As they floated by, I leaned back on the tree stump a little. I observed the trees above me along the banks. Though I could not name what kind of tree they were, I saw that they all were old and solid, with deep roots. They leaned over the water as if they were in sympathy with it, as if they listened to it and understood its murmur, its shifting currents, its deeper eddies, and its floating, lifeless bodies. The water, after all, gave the trees life. If the justice system in Chicago could somehow be resurrected to such a degree that the crimes of the wrongful conviction lawyers and activists could be revealed in a courtroom, the perpetrators might be judged and punished. The greatest offenders—even the ones who had held prestigious positions at universities—might be brought to this river. They would be taken up these trees to the most distant branches that would support them. There they might be held for some time, long enough for the bodies in the river to notice them and arise, the way they had done for me. Then the offenders could be tossed into the river to float or sink amidst their labor. Perhaps they would drown in it. The victims in the river could see this and then, finally, the burning of their wounds would cease. Then, perhaps, they could proceed to a place beyond the river.

I stood up from the tree stump, my arm reaching out to the bodies, which were closer now, showing as they got closer that they were, in fact, a collection of logs floating by, showing that I had just been imagining things again.

Chapter 16

THE LAW

A few months after meeting Simms, I was in my condo. The phone rang. I looked at the number on the caller ID. It was the front gate. I got up slowly in my ground-floor unit, went to the blinds, pressed my face between two of the slats, and peered out. There was the process server standing at the gate with the papers in his hand. As I looked at him, the phone kept ringing. This was his third attempt to get to me, but the design of my building worked to my advantage. The front gate prevented him from just walking up to my front door. Even if he talked someone into letting him in, I could see him approaching from my ground-floor window. I could rise and step back into the bathroom or bedroom, where I could not be seen from any of the windows. My back door was even more secure. It opened into a common area that was protected by walls and locked gates. If he somehow got someone to let him in and knocked on my back door, I simply didn't answer. There was no window on it. Waiting for me outside on the street until I had to leave the building didn't work either, because the back door led to an alley entrance and a parking lot where I kept my car. If he wised up and discovered this alley entrance, I could still look out between small gaps in the fence and see him before I opened the door to the alley. The truth was that I could dodge this guy forever, and that was what I planned on doing, because by this time I had become more knowledgeable in revolutionary tactics.

He remained at the front gate, making jerky movements. He paced back and forth, looking around, hoping, it seemed, he would catch me pulling up in my car. I sat back in my chair. There was some measure of pleasure in the cat-and-mouse game, but the reality of being sued and living under this siege was its own desolation and rage. I was being sued by the private investigator Paul Ciolino, who had worked with David Protess in obtaining the exoneration of Anthony Porter in 1999. Ciolino had played the central role of obtaining the "confession" of Alstory Simon, the confession that was lambasted by prosecutors when they released Simon from prison. Simon's attorneys had filed a massive $40 million lawsuit against Northwestern, Protess, and Ciolino after he was freed from prison. In response, Ciolino had filed a desperate, ludicrous countersuit, alleging a conspiracy by Bill Crawford and me, Simon's attorneys, two private investigators, and even Cook County State's Attorney Anita Alvarez. Ciolino and his attorney alleged that we had all conspired to free Simon from prison as a vendetta against Northwestern and the wrongful conviction movement.

Ciolino was demanding $26 million. Now the process server was trying to serve me with the subpoena.

I was a fugitive in my own home, and for what? Because I had helped free Alstory Simon, an innocent man. Look how far I had sunk. It started the summer before when a judge had ruled I had to give up my own emails to Flint Taylor from the People's Law Office. After that, my attorney had advised I get insurance against any further legal actions. At first I waved it off. What could I be sued for, I asked him. Truth, I reminded him, was an affirmative defense against defamation, and I would happily refute any claims that Porter or Hobley were innocent. But my lawyer kept harping on getting the insurance. So one day I marched into my insurance agent's office and purchased a policy, one that would now cover my attorney's fees in this lawsuit. Without this insurance I would be paying thousands out of my own pocket. For Bill Crawford, the retired journalist with whom I had worked on the Porter case, living on his retirement, the situation was much bleaker. Though his book about the Anthony Porter case had been written wholly on public record of court transcripts, police reports, and news articles, though it had been bolstered by a prosecutor calling for Simon's release from prison and a judge ruling that Protess and Ciolino had engaged in an elaborate ruse, Bill was thrown into the lawsuit without any insurance. He lived in quite feasible fear of a trial dragging on for months, even years, bankrupting him. Both of us believed that harassment was a primary motivation in Ciolino's lawsuit.

For both of us, too, the lawsuit was a crippling blow to our writing careers. Few publishers would consider such a

controversial narrative on the wrongful conviction movement's corruption to begin with, even when they saw clearly
it was true. But with a multimillion-dollar defamation
lawsuit now pending, it was impossible. This damage to our
reputations, in our minds, was another motive in the lawsuit:
to prevent our writing from hitting the mainstream media.
What would follow right behind this lawsuit, no doubt, was a
campaign to besmirch us in the local media, the media that
had been so complicit in cheerleading Protess's cases. A rage
descended upon us, a rage, I often thought, that the detectives who had been falsely accused of coercing confessions
lived in, a rage, I was learning, as elemental to the city as its
landscape.

Something outside my window caught my eye. The
process server had talked someone in the building into
letting him in. He was walking toward my entrance. I
grabbed my cell phone and retreated into the bathroom, and
waited. Then I thought, what the hell, I might as well take my
morning constitutional while I was there, so I sat down on
the toilet. The buzzer went off, two short and then several
long ones.

"Go fuck yourself," I said out loud.

The buzzer went off again, another long one. I thought I
could hear the guy cursing, but that was impossible. On the
wall of the bathroom opposite, I had taped up favorite quotes
from writers, writing ideas, and a few notes from people I
loved—passages I would glance at after I took a shower and
got ready for work. Here was one by Walt Whitman, above
me now as I sat on the toilet, defecating while someone was

at my door with a subpoena about a double murder thirty years earlier.

> After continued personal ambition and effort, as a
> young fellow, to enter with the rest into competition for
> the usual rewards, business, political, literary, &c.—to
> take part in the great mêlée, both for victory's prize
> itself and to do some good—After years of those aims
> and pursuits, I found myself remaining possess'd, at the
> age of thirty-one to thirty-three, with a special desire
> and conviction. Or rather, to be quite exact, a desire that
> had been flitting through my previous life, or hovering
> on the flanks, mostly indefinite hitherto, had steadily
> advanced to the front, defined itself, and finally domi-
> nated everything else. This was a feeling or ambition to
> articulate and faithfully express in literary or poetic
> form, and uncompromisingly, my own physical,
> emotional, moral, intellectual, and æsthetic Personality,
> in the midst of, and tallying, the momentous spirit and
> facts of its immediate days, and of current America—
> and to exploit that Personality, identified with place
> and date, in a far more candid and comprehensive
> sense than any hitherto poem or book.....

That's what I wanted to do. Now look at me. Another few buzzes, then I heard the door of my building open, a sign he was leaving. All was still in my condo, so still it seemed that even my cats in the other room were not moving. The quiet was shattered by a loud banging on my window, followed by a voice shouting "Martin Preib, Martin Preib," but mispronouncing my last name. My cats, alarmed, jumped down and ran into the bathroom with me, two of them rubbing up against my leg. I reached down to pet them. This motherfucker was now pounding on the windows to my condo.

"Martin Preib, Martin Preib."

Silence.

As I sat hiding on the toilet, the quotes above me were ideals and hopes for a life that seemed more distant than ever. You are hiding in your own bathroom, sitting on a toilet, avoiding service for a multimillion-dollar lawsuit from the federal courts declaring that you are a liar, that you conspired to get Alstory Simon out of prison as a tactic of revenge, that you would release a killer as part of a massive plot to attack people you hated. The claim was that I would squander the attention I had garnered for my first book to engage in a conspiracy to undermine the wrongful conviction movement by fighting to spring a guilty Alstory Simon. I shook my head, thinking about it. I risked everything to do this—my writing career, my reputation, my job, my pension —and perhaps faced prison time? What was equally sickening was the fact that so many people would embrace such nonsense, steeped as the city was in the mythology that Taylor, Protess, and Ciolino had fought so hard to impose.

"Goddamn, motherfucking shit," I heard the process server say outside my window, then I heard his retreating steps. I got up from the toilet, washed up quietly, then peered slowly around the hallway wall next to my bathroom. He could still be hiding in the courtyard. Slowly I crept back to my desk, looking into the bushes outside my window, but he had given up. The cats returned as well, lounging on the cat tree I had put by the main window. I reached out to pet them one at a time. I sat back in my chair, unable to escape the notion that my ruin was inevitable. First, I had lost the book contract with the University of Chicago Press, forcing me to self-publish. Then I had been subpoenaed by the People's Law Office, dragged into court so they could see my emails with former commander Jon Burge. Now, a year later, I was being served with a civil lawsuit demanding $26 million by a man who was accused in a federal lawsuit of helping to engineer what Simon's attorneys alleged was one of the most macabre plots in the history of the city. Ciolino, confronted by a prosecutor and a judge with his alleged misdeeds, merely doubled-down on his attack, employing the tactics that had served him so well for decades, and launched a legal case against us. He announced his counter-lawsuit in a press conference covered by all the local media. It was clear many of them wished he would prevail, because they had bought into his lies about wrongful conviction cases. How could the Chicago media bear the ignominy of thirty years' worth of letting killers out?

What confounded me most was the absence of shame among Ciolino and his supporters. Confronted with so much evidence that his plot to get Porter out of prison was a fraud, the media, Northwestern, Protess, and Ciolino made no public apology that they had fought for the release of a man who shot two human beings down in a park. More so, no one in the city, particularly the media, followed the evidence of corruption in the Porter case to others, including the Hobley case. This was key and, in my mind, the real reason Ciolino was attacking us. Ciolino served as a bridge between the corruption in the Porter case to Hobley's.

Here is why. The central witness in the 1987 Hobley arson, Andre Council—who had witnessed Hobley purchase the gas, fill the gas can, and then walk back in the direction of the apartment building shortly before the fire—came forward to describe an incredible scenario. He testified that in 2000 he was at his home one morning when Ciolino and one of Hobley's attorneys from DePaul University, a prominent wrongful conviction attorney named Andrea Lyon, came to his door. Council stated that the two offered him free tuition for his daughter at DePaul if he would change his testimony about witnessing Hobley buy the gas. One of the most disturbing aspects of Council's claim was that it matched the statements of witnesses in the Porter case, who also claimed that Ciolino and Protess had offered bribes in exchange for changed testimony. These allegations of bribing and manipulating witness statements by Ciolino now surfaced in independent cases, from witnesses who did not know each other. And that wasn't the end of it. In their massive lawsuit, Simon's attorneys alleged a pattern of misconduct, including bribed statements, not just in the Porter and Hobley cases, but in many others, spanning decades. In a civil trial, all this could come out.

Where was the outrage? Where was anger at the injustices coming out in these cases? It was a mark of what influence this movement had had upon the country that such a countersuit could not be laughed out of the courts, ridiculed in the media, that the Feds would not take up an investigation in response to it. Some motherfucker was knocking on my window trying to serve me a subpoena? I considered retaliation. Violent images came to mind. *I got a subpoena for you, bitch.* Suddenly I noticed I was sweating. My heart was racing. My own misguided life rose up before me, the fact that I had lived so much of it under dangerous delusions. I had been a lousy friend, a lousy son, a coward. I had wasted so much. The law, I had come to believe, had offered the possibility of recognizing such darkness, then atoning for it. I hoped that, as both a cop and a writer, I might employ it as a means of discovery, the way the wrongful conviction activists, even the writers like Márquez and the magical realists, had employed Marxist revolution as the underpinnings of their own imaginative lives. But such notions about the law might be little more than vanity on my part. In Chicago, I knew from experience, trying to move toward the light only moves one to the darkness. That was the city's essential corruption, its elemental fraud. Look at the students at Northwestern who had followed Protess. Look at the journalists who had given voice to the claim that Hobley was innocent without doing any real investigation. Look at what darkness they lived in. Look at me.

It was in this deflated frame of mind, this desolation, that I looked up and noticed the day had moved into late afternoon. It was early autumn. Indifferent now to the presence of a process server, indifferent to the entire legal case and my role in it, I rose. I went out the front door to the private beach along Lake Michigan behind our building. Bright blue waves were crashing against the rocks, turning white. I went to the edge, to the small fence at the outskirts of the lawn where I could look out over the water. The challenge of being a cop in Chicago, and a writer, was maintaining some humanity in the face of what the city truly was. Perhaps this was one reason I was drawn to wrongful conviction cases, for they seemed to point to a power in the city to exert itself into the other world, to hold the murder victims in its grasp, for its own ends, and to tell a story about them so false, so corrupt, yet one that endures in the city's institutions. These narratives must be an affront to the other world. Perhaps not. Perhaps Chicago is the essential reality, the way things are in this world and the other. Perhaps the cruelty and brutality of the city is a slight reflection of the horror to come. " 'What dreams may come,' " I said out loud, and I sat down on a chair, exhausted. Perhaps, I wondered as I became more and more drowsy, the magical release of killers like Porter and Hobley was the merging of the magical and realism in its truest essence, stripped of its ideological guise. I pulled my jacket up around my neck, sank lower in the chair, and let my head fall to the side. I propped it up with my arm, my elbow resting on the arm of the chair, perhaps the last time I would be able to nod off outside before the cold weather came. This nodding off by the lake, a sign that I am getting old. And I slept.

My dead body lingered offshore, the current that once pulled it away now ceased. I did not know that the dead, with their diminished locomotion, could feel a sense of duty, conviction even. I always figured the dead no longer gave a fuck, but that wasn't the case. Floating in the water, I suddenly knew so much about the dead. They see the world with an amazing clarity, with absolutes totally impossible for the living. They know how dangerous such absolutes are for the living, how wrongheaded. That's why there are juries, strict rules of evidence, endless appeals, different courts. To the dead, these processes, when sincere, are holy. They are a form of prayer. This is why the dead love the law, I realized as I floated offshore. The law is a gift to the living, one the dead try to pass along to the living as a kind of life jacket, if the living will only accept it. The dead honor the living who move toward the law, even when the living are groping in the dark and totally wrong, for the dead believe there is honor merely in the impulse.

The dead disdain anyone trying to turn the law into a tool of their private design. I knew, because the dead who exist under the burden of such designs are held suspended. I could suddenly see their bodies all around me in the lake, so many I could not count. They were not filthy or diseased; they were not even ugly to me. Many—like Jerry Hillard and Marilyn Green, Philip and Anita Hobley—were near to me, and I could easily recognize them. Many others I did not know, but knew I would someday. That was why I became a writer, why I fused the calling of a cop with an imaginative life, to sort out these bodies, name them, and give them a narrative. This would be the fulfillment of the law. These bodies were, like me, waiting for a narrative that was true, that was lawful. Until that time came, every word, every false claim spoken over them was a sin, an awful, terrifying sin.

My dead body felt some small waves picking me up and moving me back toward the shore. Unlike before, I didn't fight it or lament it, though it was incredibly sad and foreboding. I sensed with some conviction that my ruin in the city was also my salvation, and that I might see my father and mother again, all my loved ones, and that there would be forgiveness and understanding with all of them, even with my enemies. It was an irresistible thought, and I was suddenly overwhelmingly grateful for a wave that picked me up and pushed me back toward the shore, grateful, too, that I had become a cop when I was living.

Made in the USA
Monee, IL
09 July 2021